BANKS AND BANKING DEVELOPMENTS

BANK REGULATION

PROPOSED RELIEF LEGISLATION AND BURDEN ON SMALL BANKS

Banks and Banking Developments

Additional books in this series can be found on Nova's website
under the Series tab.

Additional e-books in this series can be found on Nova's website
under the eBooks tab.

BANKS AND BANKING DEVELOPMENTS

BANK REGULATION

PROPOSED RELIEF LEGISLATION AND BURDEN ON SMALL BANKS

MIRANDA SCHMIDT
EDITOR

nova publishers
New York

Library of Congress Cataloging-in-Publication Data

ISBN: 978-1-63485-520-4

Published by Nova Science Publishers, Inc. † New York

CONTENTS

PREFACE

The 114th Congress is considering legislation to provide "regulatory relief" for banks. The need for such relief, some argue, results from the increased regulation that was applied in response to vulnerabilities that became evident during the financial crisis that began in 2007. In the aftermath of the crisis, the Dodd-Frank Wall Street Reform and Consumer Protection Act (Dodd-Frank Act), a wide-ranging package of regulatory reform legislation, was enacted. Bank failures spiked during the crisis, and changes to banking regulation were a key part of financial reform. As financial regulators have implemented the Dodd-Frank Act and other reforms, some in Congress claim that the pendulum has swung too far toward excessive regulation. They argue that the additional regulation has resulted in significant costs that have stymied economic growth and restricted consumers' access to credit. Others, however, contend the current regulatory structure has strengthened financial stability and increased protections for consumers. They are concerned that regulatory relief for banks could negatively affect consumers and market stability. This book assesses banking regulatory relief proposals contained in bills that have been marked up by committee or have seen floor action in the 114th Congress; explains the concept of regulatory burden and the different ways it can be manifested; analyzes whether small banks are relatively more burdened by regulation than big banks; and evaluates rationales for reducing the regulatory burden on small banks relative to large banks, policy approaches to do so, and the potential consequences on other market participants of providing relief to small banks.

In: Bank Regulation
Editor: Miranda Schmidt
ISBN: 978-1-63485-520-4

Chapter 1

"REGULATORY RELIEF" FOR BANKING: SELECTED LEGISLATION IN THE 114TH CONGRESS*

Sean M. Hoskins, Raj Gnanarajah, Marc Labonte, Edward V. Murphy and Gary Shorter

SUMMARY

The 114th Congress is considering legislation to provide "regulatory relief" for banks. The need for this relief, some argue, results from new regulations introduced in response to vulnerabilities that were identified during the financial crisis that began in 2007. Some have contended that the increased regulatory burden—the cost associated with government regulation and its implementation—is resulting in significant costs that restrain economic growth and consumers' access to credit. Others, however, believe the current regulatory structure strengthens financial stability and increases protections for consumers, and they are concerned that regulatory relief for banks could negatively affect consumers and market stability. Regulatory relief proposals, therefore, may involve a trade-off between reducing costs associated with regulatory burden and reducing benefits of regulation.

---

* This is an edited, reformatted and augmented version of a Congressional Research Service, Publication No. R44035, dated February 11, 2016.

This report discusses regulatory relief legislation for banks in the 114th Congress that, at the time this report was published, has seen floor action or has been ordered to be reported by a committee. Many, but not all, of the bills would make changes to the Dodd-Frank Act (P.L. 111- 203), wide ranging financial reform enacted in response to the financial crisis.

The bills analyzed in this report would provide targeted regulatory relief in a number of different areas:

- **Safety and Soundness Regulations.** Safety and soundness, or prudential, regulation is designed to ensure that a bank maintains profitability and avoids failure. After many banks failed during the financial crisis, the reforms implemented in the wake of the crisis were intended to make banks less likely to fail. While some view these efforts as essential to ensuring that the banking system is safe, others view the reforms as having gone too far and imposing excessive costs on banks. Critics of the status quo have proposed several bills to reduce the burden associated with safety and soundness regulations.
- **Mortgage and Consumer Protection Regulations.** Several bills would modify regulations issued by the Consumer Financial Protection Bureau (CFPB), a regulator created by the Dodd-Frank Act to provide an increased regulatory emphasis on consumer protection. The Dodd-Frank Act gave the CFPB new authority and transferred existing authorities to it from the banking regulators. Many regulatory relief proposals could be viewed in light of a broader policy debate about whether the CFPB has struck the appropriate balance between consumer protection and regulatory burden and whether congressional action is needed to achieve a more desirable balance. One legislative focus has been several mortgage-related CFPB rulemakings pursuant to the Dodd-Frank Act.
- **Supervision and Enforcement.** *Supervision* refers to regulators' power to examine banks, instruct banks to modify their behaviors, and to impose reporting requirements on banks to ensure compliance with rules. *Enforcement* is the authority to take certain legal actions, such as impose fines, against an institution that fails to comply with rules and laws. Although regulators generally view their supervisory and enforcement actions as striking the appropriate balance between ensuring that institutions are well managed and minimizing the burden facing banks, others believe the regulators are overreaching and

preventing banks from serving their customers and therefore have introduced legislation to address these concerns.

- **Capital Issuance.** Banks are partly funded by issuing capital to investors. Disclosure requirements and investor protections may better inform investors about the risks that they are assuming but can make it more costly for institutions to raise capital. Whereas some view these existing regulatory requirements as important safeguards that ensure investors are making educated decisions, others see them as unnecessary red tape that stymies capital formation. The capital issuance legislative proposals discussed in this report are generally geared toward making it easier for financial institutions to raise funds.

Congress faces the question of how much discretion to give regulators in granting relief. Some bills leave it up to the regulators to determine how much relief should be granted, whereas others make relief mandatory. Some bills provide relief in areas regulators have already reduced regulatory burden. Some of the legislation is focused on providing relief for small banks, whereas other bills provide relief to the entire industry.

INTRODUCTION

The 114th Congress is considering legislation to provide "regulatory relief" for banks.[1] The need for such relief, some argue, results from the increased regulation that was applied in response to vulnerabilities that became evident during the financial crisis that began in 2007. In the aftermath of the crisis, the Dodd-Frank Wall Street Reform and Consumer Protection Act (Dodd-Frank Act),[2] a wide-ranging package of regulatory reform legislation, was enacted.[3] Bank failures spiked during the crisis, and changes to banking regulation were a key part of financial reform. As financial regulators have implemented the Dodd-Frank Act and other reforms, some in Congress claim that the pendulum has swung too far toward excessive regulation. They argue that the additional regulation has resulted in significant costs that have stymied economic growth and restricted consumers' access to credit. Others, however, contend the current regulatory structure has strengthened financial stability and increased protections for consumers. They are concerned that regulatory relief for banks could negatively affect consumers and market stability.

This report assesses banking regulatory relief proposals contained in bills that have been marked up by committee or have seen floor action in the 114th

Congress. In the House, proposals have generally been considered in individual bills. In the Senate, proposals have been combined into one legislative package, the Financial Regulatory Improvement Act (S. 1484/S. 1910). Several proposals were also included in the version of H.R. 22, the Fixing America's Surface Transportation Act, which was signed into law as P.L. 114-94 on December 4, 2015.

The Financial Regulatory Improvement Act

The Financial Regulatory Improvement Act (S. 1484) was reported by the Senate Banking Committee on June 2, 2015. It was then included, along with other provisions related to financial regulation, in the FY2016 Financial Services and General Government Appropriations Act (S. 1910), which was reported by the Senate Appropriations Committee on July 30, 2015. (Only one provision from S. 1484, related to mortgage servicing assets, was included in the Consolidated Appropriations Act of 2016 (H.R. 2029), which was signed into law as P.L. 114-113 on December 18, 2015.) The Congressional Budget Office (CBO) estimated that S. 1484 "would increase net direct spending by $284 million and reduce revenues by $93 million over the next 10 years, leading to a net increase in the deficit of $377 million over the 2016-2025 period."[4] Of the $377 million increase in the deficit, CBO attributes $213 million to an increase in "general administrative costs" and $164 million to provisions affecting systemically important financial institutions (some of which are banks[5]). CBO does not provide cost estimates for each section, so it is unclear how much of the $377 million is related to banking regulatory relief. (This report discusses only those provisions of S. 1484/S. 1910 related to regulatory relief and banking.)

Because banks are involved in many different activities, this report does not address all regulatory relief proposals that would affect each aspect of a bank's business (e.g., it does not cover proposals affecting banks' involvement in areas such as derivatives) but focuses on those proposals that address the traditional areas of banking, such as taking deposits and offering loans.[6] Although many of the proposals would modify regulations issued after the crisis, some would adjust policies that predated the financial crisis and some proposals are characterized as technical fixes. Further, the report covers only the regulatory relief banking legislation that has seen legislative action.

The proposals discussed in this report vary with regard to the type of relief, including to whom relief would be provided and the manner in which it would be provided. For organizational purposes, this report classifies regulatory relief proposals into the categories of safety and soundness, mortgage and consumer protection, supervision and enforcement, or capital issuance. For each proposal, the report explains what the bill would do and the main arguments offered by its supporters and opponents.

Regulatory Burden

In assessing whether regulatory relief is called for or whether a regulation has not gone far enough, a central question is whether an appropriate trade-off has been struck between the benefits and costs of regulation. The different objectives and potential benefits of financial regulation include enhancing the safety and soundness of certain institutions; protecting consumers and investors from fraud, manipulation, and discrimination; and promoting financial stability while reducing systemic risk. The costs associated with government regulation are referred to as *regulatory burden*. The presence of regulatory burden does not necessarily mean that a regulation is undesirable or should be repealed. A regulation can have benefits that could outweigh its costs, but the presence of costs means, tautologically, that there is regulatory burden. Regulatory requirements often are imposed on the providers of financial services, so banks frequently are the focus of discussions about regulatory burden. But some costs of regulation are passed on to consumers, so consumers also may benefit from relief. Any benefits to banks or consumers of regulatory relief, however, would need to be balanced against a potential reduction to consumer protection and to the other benefits of regulation.

The concept of regulatory burden can be contrasted with the phrase *unduly burdensome*. Whereas regulatory burden is about the costs associated with a regulation, unduly burdensome refers to the balance between benefits and costs. For example, some would consider a regulation to be unduly burdensome if costs were in excess of benefits or the same benefits could be achieved at a lower cost. But the mere presence of regulatory burden does not mean that a regulation is unduly burdensome. Policymakers advocating for regulatory relief argue that the regulatory burden associated with certain regulations rises to the level of being unduly burdensome for banks, whereas critics of those relief proposals typically believe the benefits of regulation outweigh the regulatory burden.

Types of Regulatory Relief Proposals

As relief proposals for banks are debated, a useful framework to categorize proposals includes assessing to *whom* relief would be provided and *how* relief would be provided. Relief could be provided either to all banks to which a regulation applies or to only a subset of banks based on size, type, or the activities the banks perform. The perceived need for relief for small banks has been emphasized in the 114th Congress, and **Table 1** summarizes legislative proposals in this report that have a size threshold. Often in the regulatory relief debate, small banks are characterized as "community banks," although there is no consensus on what size threshold divides small banks from large or what are the defining characteristics of a community bank.[7]

Table 1. Selected Legislative Proposals Changing a Size Threshold

Topic	Bill Number	Proposed Exemption Level
Volcker Rule—Community Bank Exemption	S. 1484/S. 1910	$10 billion in assets, indexed to GDP
Thresholds for Enhanced Regulation	S. 1484/S. 1910	$500 billion in assets, with a designation process for entities between $50 billion and $500 billion in assets
Thresholds for Enhanced Regulation	H.R. 1309	Replaces $50 billion threshold with a designation process unless entity has already been designated by the Financial Stability Board
Regulators' Exemptive Authority	S. 1910	$10 billion in assets
Small Bank Holding Company	H.R. 3791	$5 billion in assets
Exam Frequency	S. 1484/S. 1910, H.R. 1553	$200 million, $1 billion in assets
CFPB Supervisory Threshold	S. 1484/S. 1910	$50 billion in assets
Escrow	H.R. 1529	$10 billion in assets
Mortgage Servicing	H.R. 1529	Service 20,000 mortgages
Holding Company Threshold Equalization	S. 1484/S. 1910, H.R. 37	SHLC with $10 million in assets and 1,200/2,000 shareholders

Source: Table created by the Congressional Research Service (CRS).

Notes: See text for details. SHLC=savings and loan holding company. Additional regulations discussed in this report have size-based thresholds, but Table 1 only highlights legislative proposals that would add or change exemption levels. Some of the exemption levels are indexed to gross domestic product (GDP). For more on GDP indexing, see Table A-1.

Regulatory relief can be provided in different forms, including by repealing entire provisions, by providing exemptions from specific requirements or by tailoring a requirement so that it still applies to certain entities but does so in a less burdensome way. Examples of different forms of tailoring are streamlining a regulation, grandfathering existing firms or types of instruments from a regulation, and phasing in a new regulation over time. Modifications can be made to regulations stemming from statutory requirements, regulatory or judicial interpretations of statute, or requirements originating from regulators' broad discretionary powers.

Typically, in the area of financial regulation, Congress sets the broad goals of regulation in statute and leaves it to regulators to fill in the details. Many of the legislative proposals analyzed in this report, however, would make changes to specific details of the regulation that regulators have issued. Thus, some may oppose such proposals on the grounds that Congress is overriding regulator discretion and lacks the expertise to properly make detailed, technical regulatory judgments. In some cases, Congress might nevertheless determine that narrow intervention is justified because regulators have misinterpreted its will or are not considering other relevant policy objectives.

Safety and Soundness Regulations

The goal of safety and soundness (or prudential) regulation is to ensure that a bank maintains profitability and avoids failure. The rationale for safety and soundness regulation is to protect taxpayers (who backstop federal deposit insurance) and to maintain financial stability. Regulators monitor the bank's risk profile and set various metrics that banks must maintain in areas such as capital and liquidity. After the spike in bank failures surrounding the crisis, many of the reforms implemented in the wake of the financial crisis were intended to make banks less likely to fail. Whereas some view these efforts as essential to ensuring the banking system is safe, others view the reforms as having gone too far and imposing excessive costs on banks.

Volcker Rule[8]

Section 619 of the Dodd-Frank Act, also known as the "Volcker Rule," has two main parts—it prohibits banks from proprietary trading of "risky" assets and from "certain relationships" with risky investment funds, including acquiring or retaining "any equity, partnership, or other ownership interest in or sponsor a hedge fund or a private equity fund."[9] The statute carves out exemptions from the rule for trading activities that Congress viewed as legitimate for banks to participate in, such as risk-mitigating hedging and market-making related to broker-dealer activities. It also exempts certain securities, including those issued by the federal government, government agencies, states, and municipalities, from the ban on proprietary trading.[10] The final rule implementing the Volcker Rule was adopted on January 31, 2014.[11]

Exemption for Community Banks (S. 1484/S. 1910)

Section 115 of S. 1484 (Section 916 of S. 1910) would exempt banks with total consolidated assets of $10 billion or less (indexed in future years to the growth in GDP) from the Volcker Rule. Despite the exemption, regulators would be given discretion to apply the Volcker Rule to individual small banks if they determine that the bank's activities are "inconsistent with traditional banking activities or due to their nature or volume pose a risk to the safety and soundness of the insured depository institution."

Background

Banks of all sizes must comply with the Volcker Rule, but regulators have adopted streamlined compliance requirements for banks with less than $10 billion in assets. Small banks with activities covered by the Volcker Rule can meet the requirements of the rule within existing compliance policies and procedures. However, according to the FDIC's guidance for community banks accompanying the Volcker Rule,

> The vast majority of these community banks have little or no involvement in prohibited proprietary trading or investment activities in covered funds. Accordingly, community banks do not have any compliance obligations under the Final Rule if they do not engage in any covered activities other than trading in certain government, agency, State or municipal obligations.[12]

Policy Discussion

Regulators contend that "the vast majority of community banks" who do not face compliance obligations do not face excessive burden. Banks argue that the act of evaluating the Volcker Rule to ensure that they are in compliance is burdensome in and of itself.

The fact that the vast majority of community banks do not engage in activities subject to the Volcker Rule has been used by different bank regulatory officials as a rationale to support and oppose an exemption from the Volcker Rule for small banks. On the one hand, Federal Reserve (Fed) Governor Daniel Tarullo argued in favor of an exemption on the grounds that "both community banks and supervisors would benefit from not having to focus on formal compliance with regulation of matters that are unlikely to pose problems at smaller banks."[13] On the other hand, Federal Deposit Insurance Corporation (FDIC) Vice Chairman Thomas Hoenig says that among community banks subject to compliance requirements, those with traditional hedging activities can comply simply by having clear policies and procedures in place that can be reviewed during the normal examination process. Of the remainder, he estimates that the number of community banks facing significant compliance costs represent "less than 400 of a total of approximately 6,400 smaller banks in the U.S. And of these 400, most will find that their trading-like activities are already exempt from the Volcker Rule. If the remainder of these banks have the expertise to engage in complex trading, they should also have the expertise to comply with Volcker Rule." He concludes that

> On balance, therefore, a blanket exemption for smaller institutions to engage in proprietary trading and yet be exempt from the Volcker Rule is unwise. A blanket exemption would provide no meaningful regulatory burden relief for the vast majority of community banks that do not engage at all in the activities that the Volcker Rule restricts. However, a blanket exemption for this subset of banks would invite the group to use taxpayer subsidized funds to engage in proprietary trading and investment activities that should be conducted in the marketplace, outside of the [federal] safety net.[14]

CLOs and the Volcker Rule (H.R. 37)

The Promoting Job Creation and Reducing Small Business Burdens Act (H.R. 37) passed the House on January 14, 2015. Title VIII of H.R. 37 would modify a provision of the final rule implementing the Volcker Rule. It would modify the Volcker Rule's treatment of certain collateralized loan obligations (CLOs) as impermissible covered fund investments. It would allow banks with investments in certain CLOs issued before January 31, 2014, an additional two years, until July 21, 2019, to be in compliance with the Volcker Rule.

Background

H.R. 37 involves the part of the Volcker Rule prohibiting "certain relationships" with "risky" investment funds. A CLO is a form of securitization in which a pool of loans (typically, commercial loans) is funded by issuing securities. CLOs provide nearly $300 billion in financing to U.S. companies.[15] In the final rule implementing the Volcker Rule, many of the trusts used to facilitate CLOs were included in the definition of risky investment funds. As a result, banks would have to divest themselves of certain CLO-related securities if the securities conveyed an impermissible interest in the trust. The Volcker Rule does not ban CLOs or banking organizations from holding CLOs; rather, it prohibits banking organizations from owning securities conferring ownership-like rights in CLOs.

Regulators already have exercised their discretion to extend the conformance period for banks to divest themselves of these CLO-related assets to 2016 and could extend it again until 2017. An extension beyond 2017 could require additional agency findings. H.R. 37 would extend the conformance period to 2019 for CLOs.[16] H.R. 37 applies only to banks that hold securities issued by existing CLOs funded by commercial loans. It would limit the extension period for conformance to those CLO securities issued prior to January 31, 2014. Going forward, bank participation in newly issued CLOs would have to be structured to comply with the Volcker Rule's prohibition of bank interests in risky investment firms.[17]

Policy Discussion

The potential economic impact of H.R. 37 depends on the characteristics of CLO-related obligations already held in the banking system. If banks did not expect their CLO holdings to be prohibited by the Volcker Rule, they may not have made any preparations to comply with it. Thus, proponents of extending the conformance period argue that rapid divestiture of CLO-related securities could force banks to sell these securities at a loss, perhaps in fire sales, if an extension is not granted. They argue that such stress in the banking system may curtail credit available to small- and medium-sized commercial businesses.[18]

Opponents of Title VIII of H.R. 37, including the White House, argue that extending the conformance period would undermine the intent of the Volcker Rule and allow risky securities to remain in the banking system. They contend that it could result in future destabilizing losses for banks that hold risky securities.[19] By contrast, H.R. 37 merely changes the grandfathering date of existing commercial loan-related CLO securities from 2017 to 2019. It would neither prohibit conforming CLO securities from being created in the future to fund small and medium businesses nor exempt newly issued CLOs from the Volcker Rule going forward.

Change to the "Collins Amendment" (H.R. 22, S. 1484/S. 1910)[20]

The "Collins Amendment," Section 171 of the Dodd-Frank Act, requires bank holding companies, thrift holding companies, and non-bank "systemically important financial institutions" (SIFIs) to have capital and leverage requirements at the holding company level that are no lower than those applied at the depository subsidiary. As a result, certain capital instruments, such as trust preferred securities, that had previously counted toward certain capital requirements at the holding company level would no longer be eligible. The Collins Amendment allowed capital instruments that were otherwise no longer eligible to receive grandfathered treatment if they were issued before May 19, 2010. For institutions with more than $15 billion in assets as of December 31, 2009, the instruments would be grandfathered until January 1, 2016. For institutions with less than $15 billion in assets, instruments issued before May 19, 2010, would be permanently grandfathered.[21] For institutions with less than $1 billion (those subject to the Small Bank Holding Company policy), capital instruments issued on any (past or future) date would be eligible for capital requirements.

Section 123 of S. 1484 (Section 924 of S. 1910) would change the date for determining whether banks were above the $15 billion threshold from December 31, 2009, to "December 31, 2009 or March 31, 2010." A similar provision was included in the Fixing America's Surface Transportation Act (H.R. 22/P.L. 114-94). According to testimony from Emigrant Bank, this statutory change will make its capital instruments eligible to be grandfathered from the Collins Amendment.[22]

Exemptive Authority (S. 1910)[23]

Section 928 of S. 1910[24] would give the banking regulators discretion to exempt any bank or thrift, at the subsidiary or holding company level, with less than $10 billion in assets from any rule issued by the regulators or any provision of banking law. Regulators could exempt banks on the grounds that the provision or rule is unduly burdensome, is unnecessary to promote safety and soundness, and is in the public interest. Currently, regulators may carve out a size exemption depending on whether the relevant provision of law permits it.[25]

Policy Discussion

Granting regulators more discretion to provide exemptions could be useful if it is believed that more specialized, technical expertise is required than Congress possesses to identify when policies are unduly burdensome or when exemptions would undermine the broad goals of regulation.

An alternative view is that regulatory relief involves policy tradeoffs that Congress is better placed to make than regulators. Granting regulators discretion to provide relief could result in more or less regulatory relief than Congress intended—indeed, it does not guarantee that any regulatory relief will occur. In some cases, by granting exemptions, regulators would be overriding the will of Congress, who expressly declined to include size exemptions when provisions were originally enacted.

Capital Treatment of Mortgage Servicing Assets (H.R. 1408, H.R. 2029, and S. 1484/S. 1910)[26]

The Mortgage Servicing Asset Capital Requirements Act of 2015 (H.R. 1408) was agreed to by voice vote in the House on July 14, 2015. It was then included as Section 634 of Division E of the Consolidated Appropriations Act of 2016 (H.R. 2029), which was signed into law as P.L. 114-113 on December 18, 2015. Section 116 of S. 1484 (Section 917 of S. 1910) is also similar in content to H.R. 1408. The bills would require the federal banking regulators—the Federal Reserve, Office of the Comptroller of the Currency, Federal Deposit Insurance Corporation, and National Credit Union Administration—to "conduct a study of the appropriate capital requirements for mortgage servicing assets for banking institutions."[27] H.R. 1408 as introduced would have delayed the implementation of Basel III for all but the largest institutions until the study was completed, but that provision was removed prior to House passage.

Mortgage Servicing Assets

Mortgage servicers collect payments from borrowers that are current and forward them to mortgage holders, work with borrowers that are delinquent to try to get them current, and extinguish mortgages (such as through foreclosures) if a borrower is in default. A mortgage servicer is compensated for its work. A mortgage holder can service the mortgage itself or hire an agent to act on its behalf. Just as the mortgage holder can sell the mortgage and the right to receive the stream of payments associated with a mortgage to a different investor, a servicer can sell to a different servicer the right to service a mortgage and to receive the compensation for doing so, which can make mortgage servicing a valuable asset. A *mortgage servicing asset* (MSA), therefore, is an asset that results "from contracts to service loans secured by real estate, where such loans are owned by third parties."[28] Some banks will originate a mortgage and sell the mortgage to a different investor but retain the servicing of the mortgage (so they keep the MSA) to maintain their relationship with the customer.

Banks are required to fund their assets with a certain amount of capital to protect against the possibility that their assets may drop in value. The riskier an asset, the more capital a bank is required to hold to guard against losses. The Basel III framework is an international agreement with U.S. participation that includes guidelines on how banks should be regulated, such as how much capital they are required to hold against certain assets.[29] The federal bank regulators have issued rules generally implementing the Basel III framework and setting capital requirements that banks must follow.[30] Banks have identified the capital treatment for MSAs as one of the more costly aspects of the new capital requirements.

Policy Discussion

The new capital requirements mandate more capital for MSAs, making it more costly for banks to hold MSAs. As a result, some banks have started selling their MSAs and nonbanks (financial institutions that do not accept deposits and are not subject to the Basel III capital requirements) have purchased MSAs.[31] Although the CFPB regulates nonbank mortgage servicers to ensure that they comply with consumer protections,[32] some are worried that the growth of nonbank servicers and the sale of MSAs may "trigger a race to the bottom that puts homeowners at risk" as nonbank servicers cut costs to compete for business.[33]

Given the concerns about the effect the Basel III capital requirements are having on the mortgage servicing market, some argue that "there needs to be additional review of whether or not additional capital is required simply for mortgage servicing."[34] Supporters of additional review note that Basel III is an international agreement but that MSAs are a product of the U.S. housing finance system, which is different than the housing finance system in other countries. As a result, they contend that additional study needs to be given to this unique topic.[35]

Some Members of Congress acknowledge that servicing has migrated to nonbanks and have expressed concerns about the implications of that migration. They have stated that they are generally supportive of having a study, but do not want the study to result in the delayed implementation of the Basel III requirements.[36] Critics of H.R. 1408 supported the removal of the provision in H.R. 1408 that would have delayed the implementation of Basel III for all but the largest institutions until the study was completed. They contend Basel III is important to the safety and soundness of the banking system.[37]

CBO estimates that H.R. 1408 as ordered to be reported would affect direct spending and revenues but that "the net effect on the federal budget over the next 10 years would not be significant."[38]

Thresholds for Enhanced Regulation (H.R. 1309, S. 1484/S. 1910)[39]

To address the "too big to fail" problem, Title I of the Dodd-Frank Act created an enhanced prudential regulatory regime for all large bank holding companies (BHCs) and non-bank SIFIs. Under Subtitle C of Title I, the Fed is the prudential regulator for any BHC with total consolidated assets of more than $50 billion and any firm that the Financial Stability Oversight Council (FSOC) has designated as a SIFI.[40] The Fed, with the FSOC's advice, is required to set safety and soundness standards that are more stringent than those applicable to other non-bank financial firms and BHCs that do not pose a systemic risk. There are currently about 30 U.S. BHCs with more than $50 billion in consolidated assets.[41]

Section 201 of S. 1484 (Section 931 of S. 1910) would raise the asset threshold from $50 billion to $500 billion under which BHCs are automatically subject to Title I's enhanced prudential regulation by the Fed. For BHCs with assets between $50 billion and $500 billion, FSOC would have the authority to designate them as systemically important and thus subject to enhanced prudential regulation. Under current law, the asset threshold is fixed at $50 billion, but FSOC and Fed have the discretion to raise it, whereas [42] under S. 1484/S. 1910, these thresholds would be indexed annually based on the growth rate of GDP. For a BHC to be designated, at least two-thirds of FSOC voting members, including the chairman (the Treasury Secretary), would have to find that the BHC is systemically important based initially on five factors specified by the bill and a multi-step designation process laid out in the bill. As discussed below, a FSOC designation process is already used for non-bank financial firms; compared with statute governing the current non-bank designation process, S. 1484/S. 1910 would require FSOC to provide more information to (bank or non-bank) institutions and would give institutions more opportunities to take actions to avoid or reverse a SIFI designation. It would increase public disclosure requirements surrounding the designation process, including the identity of firms under consideration for designation.[43]

S. 1484/S. 1910 would also amend provisions of the Dodd-Frank Act that apply to BHCs with more than $50 billion in assets to apply instead to BHCs subject to the revised enhanced supervision (e.g., changing who is subject to emergency divestiture powers and to fees that finance enhanced regulation and the Office of Financial Research) Section 202 of S. 1484 (Section 932 of S. 1910) would increase the thresholds from $10 billion to $50 billion for requiring a BHC to form a risk committee (if the BHC is publicly-traded) and conduct company-run stress tests. All of these thresholds would be indexed in future years based on GDP growth. These changes would become effective 180 days after enactment.

Section 506 of S. 1484 (Section 966 of S. 1910) would require GAO to conduct a study of the Fed's enhanced regulatory regime for banks and non-banks.

H.R. 1309 was ordered to be reported by the House Financial Services Committee on November 4, 2015. It would remove the $50 billion asset threshold under which BHCs are automatically subject to Title I's enhanced prudential regulation by the Fed. If a bank has been designated as a "globally systemically important bank" (G-SIB) by the Financial Stability Board, it would automatically be subject to enhanced prudential regulation.[44] As of November 2015, there are 30 G-SIBs, of which 8 are headquartered in the United States.[45] For BHCs that are not G-SIBs, FSOC would have the authority to designate them as systemically important, and thus subject to enhanced prudential regulation, under the designation process currently used for non-bank SIFIs. For a BHC to be designated, at least two-thirds of FSOC's voting members, including the Treasury Secretary, would have to find that it is systemically important using "the indicator-based measurement approach established by the Basel Committee...." The bill would provide a one-year phase-in period so that firms currently subject to enhanced regulation remain subject while the designation process is proceeding.

H.R. 1309 would also modify other parts of the Dodd-Frank Act (e.g., banks subject to emergency divestiture powers and fees to finance enhanced regulation and the Office of Financial Research) that apply to BHCs with more than $50 billion in assets to apply instead to banks subject to the revised enhanced supervision.

Background

The final rule implementing parts of Subtitle C for banks was adopted in February 2014, and banks were required to be in compliance by January 1, 2015.[46] The final rule includes requirements for stress tests run by the Fed, capital planning, liquidity standards, living wills and risk management. In the event that the FSOC has determined that it poses a "grave threat" to financial stability, the final rule also requires any bank with more than $50 billion in assets to comply with a 15 to 1 debt to equity limit. Exposure limits of 25% of a company's capital per single counterparty were included in the proposed rule, but the Fed has indicated that it plans to finalize them at a later date. Enhanced capital requirements have not been required of all BHCs with $50 billion or more in assets; instead enhanced capital requirements for only the largest banks have been proposed or implemented through rules implementing Basel III.[47] This is an example of how there is already some "tiering" of regulation for large banks.[48]

A large number of foreign banks operating in the United States are also subject to the enhanced prudential regime.[49] Foreign banks operating with more than $50 billion in assets in the United States are required to set up intermediate BHCs that will be subject to heightened standards comparable to those applied to U.S. banks. Less stringent requirements apply to large foreign banks with less than $50 billion in assets in the United States.

Policy Discussion

Critics of the $50 billion asset threshold argue that many banks above that range are not systemically important. In particular, critics distinguish between "regional banks," which tend to be at the lower end of the asset range and, it is claimed, have a traditional banking business model comparable to community banks, and "Wall Street banks," a term applied to the largest, most complex organizations that tend to have significant non-bank financial activities.[50] If critics are correct that some banks that are currently subject to enhanced prudential regulation are not systemically important, then there may be little societal benefit from subjecting them to enhanced regulation, making that regulation unduly burdensome to them. Alternatively, proponents view practices such as living wills, stress tests, and risk committees as "best practices" that any well-managed bank should follow to prudentially manage risk.[51]

Many economists believe that the economic problem of "too big to fail" is really a problem of too complex or interdependent to fail. In other words, they believe policymakers are reluctant to allow a firm to fail if it is too complex to be wound down swiftly and orderly or if its failure would cause other firms to fail or would disrupt critical functions in financial markets. If firms and their creditors perceive policymakers as reluctant to allow the firms to fail, it creates incentives for those firms to take on excessive risk (known as "moral hazard"). These firms are referred to as systemically important.

Size correlates with complexity and interdependence, but not perfectly. It follows that a size threshold is unlikely to successfully capture all those—and only those—banks that are systemically important. A size threshold will capture some banks that are not systemically important if set too low or leave out some banks that are systemically important if set to high. (Alternatively, if policymakers believe that size is the paramount policy problem, then a numerical threshold is the best approach, although policymakers may debate the most appropriate number.) Size is a much simpler and more transparent metric than complexity or interdependence, however. Thus, policymakers face a tradeoff between using a simple, transparent but imperfect proxy for systemic importance, or they can try to better target enhanced regulation by evaluating banks on a case-by-case basis. A case-by-case designation process would be more time-consuming and resource-intensive, however. For example, only four non-banks were designated as SIFIs in three years under the existing process, and S. 1484/S. 1910 would add several additional formal steps to the process. Furthermore, there is no guarantee that FSOC will correctly identify systemically important BHCs since there is no definitive proof that a BHC is systemically important until it becomes distressed. Some fear that FSOC could make an incorrect judgment about a bank's systemic importance because most members of FSOC do not have banking expertise or because the Treasury Secretary has effective veto power.

Some Members of Congress have expressed concern about international agreements generally— and the Financial Stability Board's designations in particular—overriding domestic law in the areas of financial regulation. The G-SIB designation has not been referenced in an act of Congress, but some U.S. regulations have defined eligibility so that certain regulations apply only to banks with the G-SIB designation. H.R. 1309 would enshrine G-SIB designation in U.S. statute.

The Dodd-Frank Act and the EGRPRA Process (S. 1484/S. 1910)[52]

Background

Under the Economic Growth and Regulatory Paperwork Reduction Act (EGRPRA),[53] the OCC, Federal Reserve, and FDIC are required to conduct a review at least every 10 years "to identify outdated or otherwise unnecessary regulatory requirements imposed on insured depository institutions."[54] The agencies began the latest review process by seeking public comment in June 2014. In this review, the agencies are placing an emphasis on reducing the regulatory burden on community banks.[55]

Section 125 of S. 1484 (Section 926 of S. 1910) would require the Dodd-Frank Act to be included in the EGRPRA review and would require the NCUA and the Consumer Financial Protection Bureau (CFPB) to also participate. Currently, the NCUA is not required to review its regulations under EGRPRA, but has elected to do so "in keeping with the spirit of the law."[56] The CFPB is also not required to review its regulations through EGRPRA, but the "CFPB is required" by the Dodd-Frank Act "to review its significant rules and publish a report of its review no later than five years after they take effect."[57]

Policy Discussion

Initially, the banking regulators decided that "new regulations that have only recently gone into effect, or rules that we have yet to fully implement" would not be included in the current EGRPRA review.[58] The agencies argued that they were already "required to take burden into account in adopting these regulations," so including them in the EGRPRA process was unnecessary.[59] The regulators, however, later "decided to expand the scope of the EGRPRA review to cover more recent regulations."[60] The legislation would codify this decision.

Some argue that the Dodd-Frank Act should not be included in the EGRPRA review because such "a review would be premature and unwise, as many Dodd-Frank Act reforms have not even been implemented, and those that are in place have had a very limited time to make the intended impact."[61] If the Dodd-Frank regulations are to be included, critics contend that the "review should not be limited to the impact of regulation on regulated entities but must include a thorough analysis of the benefits of those rules collectively, including specifically the benefits of those rules in avoiding a future financial crisis and the costs, burdens, bailouts, and suffering that would accompany such a crisis."[62]

Supporters of the legislation argue that it is necessary to include the Dodd-Frank Act as well as the NCUA and the CFPB in the review in order to provide a more meaningful assessment of the regulatory burden facing financial institutions. In particular, they contend that the EGRPRA "review is only meaningful if we identify the biggest challenges for community banks and credit unions and provide real solutions."[63]

Municipal Bonds and the Liquidity Coverage Ratio (H.R. 2209)[64]

H.R. 2209 passed the House on February 1, 2016. The bill would require any municipal bond "that is both liquid and readily marketable...and investment grade" to be treated as a Level 2A high quality liquid asset for purposes of complying with the Liquidity Coverage Ratio (LCR) within three months of enactment. Municipal bonds are debt securities issued by state and local governments or public entities.[65] Members of Congress supporting H.R. 2209 have mainly voiced concern about the LCR's impact on the ability of states and local governments to borrow, but because the LCR is applied to banks, H.R. 2209 would also have an effect on bank profitability and riskiness. CBO estimated that the bill would have a negligible effect on the federal budget.[66]

Background

The banking regulators issued a final rule in 2014 that implements the LCR, which is part of bank liquidity standards required by Basel III and the Dodd-Frank Act.[67] In 2010, 27 countries agreed to modify the Basel Accords, which are internationally negotiated bank regulatory standards. In response to acute liquidity shortages and asset "fire sales" during the financial crisis, Basel III included liquidity standards for the first time. The Dodd-Frank Act requires heightened prudential standards, including liquidity standards, for banks with more than $50 billion in assets and non-banks that have been designated as SIFIs. The rule came into effect at the beginning of 2015 and will be fully phased in by the beginning of 2017.

The LCR applies to two sets of banks. A more stringent version (implementing Basel III) applies to the largest, internationally active banks, with at least $250 billion in assets and $10 billion in on-balance sheet foreign exposure. A less stringent version (implementing the Dodd-Frank Act) applies to depositories with $50 billion to $250 billion in assets, except for those with significant insurance or commercial operations. Fewer than 40 institutions must comply with the LCR, as of the third quarter of 2015. The rule does not apply to credit unions, community banks, foreign banks operating in the United States, or non-bank SIFIs. Regulators plan to issue liquidity regulations at a later date for large foreign banks operating in the United States and non-bank SIFIs.

The LCR aims to require banks to hold enough "high-quality liquid assets" (HQLA) to match net cash outflows over 30 days in a hypothetical market stress scenario in which an unusual number of creditors are withdrawing substantial amounts of funds.[68] An asset can qualify as a HQLA if it is less risky, has a high likelihood of remaining liquid during a crisis, is actively traded in secondary markets, is not subject to excessive price volatility, can be easily valued, and is accepted by the Fed as collateral for loans. HQLA must be "unencumbered"—for example, they cannot already be pledged as collateral in a loan. The assets that regulators have approved as HQLA include bank reserves, U.S. Treasury securities, certain securities issued by foreign governments and companies, securities issued by U.S. government-sponsored enterprises (GSEs), certain investment-grade corporate debt securities, and equities that are included in the Russell 1000 Index.

Different types of assets are relatively more or less liquid, and there is disagreement on how liquid assets need to be to qualify as HQLAs under the LCR. In the LCR, assets eligible as HQLA are assigned to one of three categories (Levels 1, 2A, and 2B). Assets assigned to the most liquid category (Level 1) receive more credit toward meeting the requirements, and assets in the least liquid category (Level 2B) receive less credit. For purposes of the LCR, Level 2A assets are subject to a 15% haircut (i.e., only 85% of their value counts toward meeting the LCR), whereas Level 2B assets are subject to a 50% haircut and may not exceed 15% of total HQLA.

In the 2014 final rule, municipal bonds did not qualify as HQLA to meet the LCR, but in May 2015, the Fed proposed a rule that would allow banks to count a limited amount of municipal debt as Level 2B HQLA for purposes of the LCR, if finalized.[69] According to the Fed,

> The proposed rule would allow investment grade, general obligation U.S. state and municipal bonds to be counted as HQLA up to certain levels if they meet the same liquidity criteria that currently apply to corporate debt securities. The limits on the amount of a state or

municipality's bonds that could qualify are based on the specific liquidity characteristics of the bonds.[70]

In the Fed's proposed rule, the amount of municipal debt eligible to be included as HQLA would be subject to various limitations, including an overall cap of 5% of a bank's total HQLA. Dedicated revenue bonds and insured municipal bonds would not be eligible as HQLA.[71] The Fed requires banks to demonstrate that a security has "a proven record as a reliable source of liquidity in repurchase or sales markets during a period of significant stress" in order for it to qualify as HQLA.

The Fed's proposed rule applies to institutions and holding companies regulated by the Fed. To date, the Office of the Comptroller of the Currency (OCC) and the Federal Deposit Insurance Corporation (FDIC) have not issued similar proposed rules allowing municipal bonds to count as HQLA for banks for whom they are the primary regulators. Thus, proponents of H.R. 2209 argue that the Fed's proposed rule alone would not significantly mitigate the perceived impact of the LCR on municipal bonds.

Analysis

To the extent that the LCR reduces the demand for bank holding companies to hold municipal securities, it would be expected to increase the borrowing costs of states and municipalities. The impact of the LCR on the municipal bond market is limited by the fact that banks' holdings of municipal bonds are limited and relatively few banks are subject to the LCR.[72] The Congressional Research Service (CRS) could not locate any data on the value of municipal securities held by banks subject to the LCR, but according to Federal Reserve data, all U.S. banks held about $490 billion of municipal securities in the third quarter of 2015, equal to 13% of the total outstanding.[73] Finally, even banks subject to the LCR are still allowed to hold municipal bonds, as long as they have a stable funding source to back their holdings.

Arguments that municipal bonds should qualify as HQLA because most pose little default risk confuses default risk, which is addressed by Basel's capital requirements, with liquidity risk, which is addressed by the LCR. The purpose of the LCR is to ensure that banks have ample assets that can be easily liquidated in a stress scenario; a municipal bond may pose very little default risk, but nevertheless be highly illiquid (i.e., hard to sell quickly). On the one hand, if the inclusion of assets that prove not to be liquid in the HQLA undermines the effectiveness of the LCR, it could increase the systemic risk posed by a large institution experiencing a run. On the other hand, further diversifying the types of assets that qualify as HQLA could reduce the risk stemming from any single asset class becoming illiquid.

If municipal bonds are included as HQLA, a challenge for regulators is how to differentiate between which municipal securities should or should not qualify. Some municipal securities are liquid in the sense that they are frequently traded, whereas others are not. According to data from the Municipal Securities Rulemaking Board, the 50 most actively traded municipal bond CUSIP (Committee on Uniform Securities Identification Procedures) numbers traded at least 1,970 times per year each, but even some of the largest CUSIPs traded less than 100 times a year in 2014.[74] Proponents of including municipal debt as HQLA claim that some municipal securities are more liquid than some assets that currently qualify as HQLA, such as corporate debt.[75] For purposes of the LCR, frequent trading may not be the only relevant characteristic of HQLA. For example, in the final rule, regulators argued that one reason why municipal bonds should not qualify as LCR is because banks cannot easily use them as collateral to access liquidity from repurchase (repo) markets.[76]

Were the Fed to finalize its proposed rule, it is unclear how many municipal securities would qualify as HQLA under the Fed's criteria. According to the Securities Industry and Financial Markets Association,

> By one calculation, only $186 billion of the nearly $3.7 trillion of outstanding bonds would be eligible to be included as HQLA. While we recognize that the Fed seeks to ensure that only the most secure and liquid segment of the market is eligible for banks' LCR compliance, we do not believe that excluding 95 percent of the market strikes the right balance.[77]

The share of municipal securities that would qualify as HQLA under H.R. 2209 would depend on subsequent rulemaking. The Fed's proposed rule differs from H.R. 2209 by classifying qualifying municipal bonds as Level 2B and Level 2A HQLA, respectively. The difference in treatment makes municipal bonds less attractive for purposes of the LCR in the Fed's proposed rule relative to H.R. 2209. In comparing the Fed's rule to H.R. 2209, a key policy question is whether municipal bonds have more in common with the other Level 2A HQLA, which include securities issued by government sponsored enterprises and foreign governments, or the other Level 2B HQLA, which include corporate bonds and equities.

Small Bank Holding Company Policy Threshold (H.R. 3791)[78]

H.R. 3791 was ordered to be reported by the House Financial Services Committee on December 9, 2015. It would increase the threshold for BHCs and thrift holding companies (THCs) subject to the Federal Reserve's Small Bank Holding Company Policy Statement[79] from those below $1 billion to those below $5 billion in assets. It would make a corresponding increase in the threshold for an institution to be exempted from the "Collins Amendment" to the Dodd-Frank Act.

Background

In general, the Fed limits the debt levels of BHCs and THCs to ensure that they are able to serve as a source of strength for their depository subsidiary. The Federal Reserve's Small Bank Holding Company Policy Statement is a regulation that allows BHCs and THCs that have less than $1 billion in assets to hold more debt at the holding company level than would otherwise be permitted by capital requirements if the debt is used to finance up to 75% of an acquisition of another bank. To qualify, the holding company may not be engaged in significant nonbank activities, may not conduct significant off balance sheet activities, and may not have a substantial amount of outstanding debt or equity securities registered with the Securities and Exchange Commission (with the exception of trust preferred securities). After the acquisition, the holding company is required to gradually reduce its debt levels over several years, and it faces restrictions on paying dividends until the debt level is reduced. This policy is motivated by recognition of differences between how small and large banks typically finance acquisitions.

Although the policy statement is limited to making it easier to fund acquisitions through debt, it has also been referenced in other parts of banking regulation. Banks subject to the policy enjoy streamlined compliance with certain requirements.[80] More recently, all BHCs and THCs subject to the Small Bank Holding Company Policy Statement are exempted from the Collins Amendment (Section 171) to the Dodd-Frank Act,[81] which subjects holding companies to the same capital and leverage requirements as their depository subsidiaries. Holding companies subject to the policy statement are also exempted from the rule applying Basel III capital requirements at the holding company level (although their depository subsidiaries are still subject to this rule).[82]

Since 1980, when the policy statement was issued, the threshold has been occasionally raised. Most recently, it was raised in the 1113th Congress from

$500 million to $1 billion and extended to cover savings and loan (thrift) holding companies by P.L. 113-250, which was signed into law on December 18, 2014. The Fed issued a final rule on April 9, 2015, implementing this statutory change.[83] The rule also extended the policy statement to apply to thrift holding companies.

Policy Discussion

Proponents view the legislation as providing well-targeted regulatory relief to banks with between $1 billion and $5 billion in assets. (As discussed previously, there is no consensus about whether banks of this size should be considered community banks.) Alternatively, the bill could be opposed on the grounds that providing relief based on size creates inefficient distortions in the allocation of credit or on the grounds that it weakens the ability of holding companies to act as a source of strength for affected banks.

Optional Expanded Charter for Thrifts (H.R. 1660)[84]

The Federal Savings Association Charter Flexibility Act of 2015 (H.R. 1660) was ordered to be reported by the House Committee on Financial Services on November 3, 2015. H.R. 1660 as ordered to be reported would allow a federal savings association (also known as federal thrifts) to operate with the same rights and duties as a national bank without having to change its charter.

A federal thrift and a national bank are types of financial institutions that typically accept deposits and make loans but have different charters that allow for different permitted activities. Historically, federal thrifts—which were established during the Great Depression when mortgage credit was tight—have focused on residential mortgage lending[85] and have faced restrictions in the other types of lending that they can perform. For example, federal thrifts are limited by statute[86] in the amount of commercial and non-residential real estate loans they can hold, whereas national banks do not face the same statutory restrictions.[87] Over time, the federal thrift charter has been expanded to allow federal thrifts to offer products similar to those offered by national banks, eroding some of the difference between the two.[88]

If a federal thrift wants to alter its business model and engage in activities that it is prohibited from performing but are allowed for a national bank, the federal thrift would have to convert its charter to a national bank charter, which can be a costly process. For federal thrifts that have mutual ownership structures, there would be a "need to convert to a stock form of ownership prior to converting to a national bank."[89] Supporters of H.R. 1660 argue that the proposal would provide federal thrifts "additional flexibility to adapt to changing economic conditions and business environments" by allowing a less costly process for expanding federal thrifts' permitted activities without having to convert charters.[90] In addition, they argue that the change would not pose a safety and soundness risk because federal thrifts are regulated by the same regulator as national banks—the OCC regulates federal thrifts and national banks—[91] and the bill would provide the OCC with authority to issue regulations as necessary to safeguard safety and soundness, ensuring that the switch would not pose undue risk. While there would be no change in regulator, the regulations and restrictions that apply to national banks would apply to federal thrifts that elected to make the change. The federal thrifts that elected to change, however, would maintain their corporate form and continue to be treated as federal thrifts for purposes of "consolidation, merger, dissolution, conversion (including conversion to a stock bank or to another charter), conservatorship, and receivership." [92]

Others who seem to support H.R. 1660 have raised issues with the bill being too narrowly focused and argue that it should also provide assistance to credit unions, which are another type of financial institution with a charter of permitted activities. Credit unions, for example, are limited in the amount of member business loans that they can hold.[93] Just as H.R. 1660 would expand the lending opportunities for thrifts, credit union supporters argue that credit unions' lending opportunities should be expanded as well.[94]

A broader issue underlying H.R. 1660 is whether the government should offer different charters, with different benefits and responsibilities, for businesses that engage in similar activities. Bills that narrow the differences between charter type arguably weaken the benefits of having different charters.

MORTGAGE AND CONSUMER PROTECTION REGULATIONS

Banks are also regulated for consumer protection. These regulations are intended to ensure the safety of the products, such as loans, that banks offer to consumers.

Several bills would modify regulations issued by the Consumer Financial Protection Bureau, a regulator created by the Dodd-Frank Act to provide an increased regulatory emphasis on consumer protection. Prior to the Dodd-

Frank Act, bank regulators were responsible for consumer protection. The Dodd-Frank Act gave the CFPB new authority and transferred existing authorities to it from the banking regulators. The Dodd-Frank Act also directed the CFPB to implement several new mortgage-related policy changes through rulemakings. The bills included in this section could be viewed in light of a broader policy debate about whether the CFPB has struck the appropriate balance between consumer protection and regulatory burden, and whether congressional action is needed to achieve a more desirable balance.

Manufactured Housing (H.R. 650 and S. 1484/S. 1910)[95]

The Preserving Access to Manufactured Housing Act of 2015 (H.R. 650) was passed by the House on April 14, 2015. H.R. 650 as passed would affect the market for manufactured housing by amending the definitions of *mortgage originator* and *high-cost mortgage* in the Truth-in-Lending Act (TILA).[96] Section 108 of S. 1484 (Section 909 of S. 1910) contains a similar provision.

Manufactured homes, which often are located in more rural areas, are a type of single-family housing that is factory built and transported to a placement site rather than constructed on-site.[97] When purchasing a manufactured home, a consumer does not necessarily have to own the land on which the manufactured home is placed. Instead, the consumer could lease the land, a practice that is different from what is often done with a site-built home.[98] Manufactured housing also differs from site-built properties in other ways, such as which consumer protection laws apply to the transaction and how state laws title manufactured housing.[99]

The Dodd-Frank Act changed the definitions for mortgage originator and high-cost mortgage to provide additional consumer protections to borrowers for most types of housing transactions, including manufactured housing. Some argue that these protections restrict credit for manufactured housing. The proposals would modify the definitions of mortgage originator and high-cost mortgage with the goal of increasing credit. Critics of the proposal are concerned about the effect on consumers of reducing the consumer protections. The first part of the proposals would not affect banks but would affect manufactured-home retailers. It is discussed briefly to provide context for the second part of the proposals, which would affect banks more directly.

Definition of Mortgage Originator

In response to problems in the mortgage market when the housing bubble burst, the Secure and Fair Enforcement for Mortgage Licensing Act of 2008 (SAFE Act)[100] and the Dodd-Frank Act established new requirements for mortgage originators' licensing, registration, compensation, training, and other practices. A mortgage originator is someone who, among other things, "(i) takes a residential mortgage loan application; (ii) assists a consumer in obtaining or applying to obtain a residential mortgage loan; or (iii) offers or negotiates terms of a residential mortgage loan."[101] The current definition in implementing the regulation excludes employees of manufactured-home retailers under certain circumstances, such as "if they do not take a consumer credit application, offer or negotiate credit terms, or advise a consumer on credit terms."[102] The legislation would expand the exception such that retailers of manufactured homes or their employees would not be considered mortgage originators unless they received more compensation for a sale that included a loan than for a sale that did not include a loan.

Policy Discussion

Supporters of the proposals argue that the current definition of mortgage originator is too broad and negatively affects the manufactured-housing market. Manufactured-home retailers "have been forced to stop providing technical assistance to consumers during the process of home buying" because of concerns that providing this assistance will result in the retailers being deemed loan originators, which in turn will lead to costs that the manufactured-home retailers do not want to bear, according to supporters.[103] Supporters of the bills argue that this situation has unnecessarily complicated the purchase process for consumers. H.R. 650 would allow manufactured-home retailers to provide minimal assistance to consumers for which they would not be compensated.

Opponents of the proposals, however, note that the existing protections are intended to prevent retailers from pressuring consumers into making their purchase through a particular creditor. Expanding the exemption, they argue, "would perpetuate the conflicts of interest and steering that plague this industry and allow lenders to pass additional costs on to consumers."[104]

High-Cost Mortgage

The proposals also would narrow the definition of high-cost mortgage for manufactured housing. A high-cost mortgage often is referred to as a "HOEPA loan" because the Home Ownership and Equity Protection Act (HOEPA)[105] provides additional consumer protections to borrowers for certain high-cost transactions involving a borrower's home. The Dodd-Frank Act expanded the protections available to high-cost mortgages by having more types of mortgage transactions be covered and by lowering the thresholds at which a mortgage would be deemed high cost. The CFPB issued a rule implementing those changes in 2013.[106]

Consumers receive additional protections on high-cost transactions, such as "special disclosure requirements and restrictions on loan terms, and borrowers in high-cost mortgages have enhanced remedies for violations of the law."[107] Prior to originating the mortgage, lenders are required to receive "written certification that the consumer has obtained counseling on the advisability of the mortgage from a counselor that is approved to provide such counseling."[108] Because of these protections and the added legal liability associated with originating a high-cost mortgage, originating a HOEPA loan is generally considered more costly for a lender (which could be either a bank or a nonbank) than originating a non-HOEPA loan. This is an example of the trade-off between consumer protection and credit availability—if a loan is deemed high-cost, the consumer has added protections, but the lender may be less willing to originate it.

A mortgage is high cost if certain thresholds are breached related to the mortgage's (1) annual percentage rate (APR) or (2) points and fees.[109]

The APR is a measure of how much a loan costs expressed as an annualized rate. Computation of the APR includes the interest rate as well as certain fees, such as compensation to the lender and other expenses. Under the *APR test*, a loan is considered to be a high-cost mortgage if the APR exceeds the average prime offer rate (APOR, an estimate of the market mortgage rate based on a survey of rates) by more than 6.5 percentage points for most mortgages or by 8.5 percentage points for certain loans under $50,000.[110] The bills would increase the threshold for the latter category to 10 percentage points above the APOR for certain transactions involving manufactured housing below $75,000.

Points and fees, the second factor, refers to certain costs associated with originating the mortgage. The term *point* refers to compensation paid up front to the lender by the borrower. A point is expressed as a percentage of the loan amount, with one point equal to 1% of the loan amount.[111] The fees included in the definition of points and fees include prepayment penalties, certain types of insurance premiums, and other real estate-related fees. Under the *points and fees test*, the mortgage is high cost if the points and fees exceed (1) 5% of the total amount borrowed for most loans in excess of $20,000 or (2) the lesser of 8% of the total amount or $1,000 for loans of less than $20,000.[112]

The proposals would create a third category for the points and fees test for manufactured-housing loans. Under the third category, certain types of manufactured-housing transactions would be deemed high cost if the points and fees on loans less than $75,000 were greater than 5% of the total loan amount or greater than $3,000. This higher threshold would make it less likely that a manufactured-housing loan would be high-cost under the points and fees test, all else equal.

Policy Discussion

Data from the Consumer Financial Protection Bureau's (CFPB's) September 2014 report on the manufactured-housing market indicate that manufactured-housing loans are more likely to be HOEPA loans than loans for traditional, site-built homes. The CFPB analyzed data for originations from 2012, which was before the more expansive Dodd-Frank definition of high-cost mortgage took effect. The CFPB estimated the share of the 2012 market that would have violated the APR test (which is just one of the high-cost triggers) had the current thresholds been in effect and found that "0.2 percent of all home-purchase loans in the U.S. have an interest rate that exceeds the HOEPA APR threshold. This fraction is only 0.01 percent for site-built homes but nearly 17 percent for manufactured homes."[113]

As the CFPB notes, this estimate of the share of HOEPA loans may *understate* the true share because it does not include the points and fees test, but it also may *overstate* the true share because lenders may have adjusted the points, fees, interest rate, profitability of the loan, and other factors so that fewer loans would have been high-cost had the new thresholds been in effect.[114] Either way, the CFPB's data are illustrative of the fact that a larger share of manufactured-housing loans than site-built loans is likely to be affected by the high-cost mortgage requirements. The CFPB stated that the changes to HOEPA made by Dodd-Frank likely would lead to a larger share of all loans being high-cost, but "the resulting increase in the share of high-cost mortgages was much larger for manufactured-housing loans than for loans on site-built homes."[115]

Manufactured-housing loans are more likely to be high-cost for several reasons. Manufactured-housing loans usually are smaller than loans for site-built properties. The CFPB's report found that the "median loan amount for site-built home purchase was $176,000, more than three times the manufactured home purchase loan median of $55,000."[116] Because manufactured-housing loans often are for a smaller amount, they are likely to have higher APR and points and fees ratios; the APR and points and fees computations include some fixed costs that do not vary proportionately to the size of the loan. All else equal, smaller loans would be more likely to breach the thresholds. To account for this, the APR test and the points and fees test have thresholds that vary based on the size of the loan, as explained above. Additionally, because of how some states title manufactured homes and other unique aspects of the manufactured-housing market, a manufactured-housing loan is likely to have a higher interest rate than a loan involving a site-built home (all else equal), which makes it more likely that the loan will violate the APR threshold.[117]

Supporters of the bills argue that the high-cost thresholds are poorly targeted for manufactured-housing loans because the fixed costs and higher rates associated with smaller manufactured-housing loans make it more likely that the thresholds will be exceeded.[118] The existing adjustments for small-dollar loans are insufficient and allow too many manufactured-housing loans to be high- cost. As a result, critics of the current threshold argue, credit will be restricted as some lenders will be less inclined to bear the expense and liability associated with originating high-cost manufactured-housing loans. H.R. 650, they claim, is important for ensuring that credit is available for borrowers who want to purchase a manufactured home.

Opponents of the legislation argue that the APR and points and fees thresholds already are adjusted for the size of the loan and do not need to be further modified. Doing so would weaken consumer protections, they argue, for borrowers who are likely to have lower incomes and be more "economically vulnerable consumers."[119] The Obama Administration has said that "if the President were presented with H.R. 650, his senior advisors would recommend that he veto the bill."[120]

CBO estimates that H.R. 650 as ordered reported "would increase direct spending by less than $500,000."[121] The bill would not affect revenues or discretionary spending.

Points and Fees (H.R. 685 and S. 1484/S. 1910)[122]

The Mortgage Choice Act of 2015 (H.R. 685) was passed by the House on April 14, 2015. H.R. 685 as passed would modify the definition of points and fees to exclude from the definition (1) insurance held in escrow and (2) certain fees paid to affiliates of the lender. S. 1484 and S. 1910 would also exclude insurance held in escrow from the definition of points and fees, but would not exclude fees paid to affiliates. Instead, Section 107 of S. 1484 (Section 908 of S. 1910) would require a study and report that would examine the effect of the Dodd-Frank Act on the ability of affiliated lenders to provide mortgage credit, on the mortgage market for mortgages that are not qualified mortgages, on the ability of prospective homeowners to obtain financing, and several other issues.

As is elaborated upon below, points and fees refers to certain costs that are paid by the borrower related to lender compensation and other expenses that are associated with originating the mortgage. How points and fees are defined can have an effect on *credit availability* (mortgage lenders argue that the current definition of points and fees makes it harder for them to extend credit) and an effect on *consumer protection* (consumer groups argue that expanding the definition could lead to borrowers being steered into more expensive mortgages that they could be less able to repay).

The Ability-to-Repay Rule and Points and Fees

The definition of points and fees is a component of multiple rules, but it is often discussed in the context of the Ability-to-Repay (ATR) rule.[123] Title XIV of the Dodd-Frank Act established the ATR requirement and instructed the CFPB to establish the definition of a qualified mortgage (QM) as part of its implementation. The ATR rule requires a lender to determine, based on documented and verified information, that at the time a mortgage loan is made the borrower has the ability to repay the loan. Failure to make such a determination could result in a lender having to pay damages to a borrower who brings a lawsuit claiming that the lender did not follow the ATR rule. This legal risk gives lenders added incentive to comply with the ATR rule.

One of the ways a lender can comply with the ATR rule is by originating a QM.[124] A QM is a mortgage that satisfies certain underwriting and product-feature requirements, such as having payments below specified debt-to-income ratios and having a term no longer than 30 years. By making a QM, a lender is presumed to have complied with the ATR rule and receives legal protections that could reduce its potential legal liability. A lender can comply with the ATR rule by making a mortgage that is not a QM, but the lender will not receive the additional legal protections. The definition of a QM, therefore, is important to a lender seeking to minimize its legal risk. Because of this legal risk, some are concerned that, at least in the short term, the vast majority of mortgages that are originated will be mortgages meeting the QM standards due to the legal protections that QMs afford lenders, even though there are other means of complying with the ATR rule.[125]

As an additional requirement for a mortgage to be a QM, certain points and fees associated with the mortgage must be below specified thresholds. Some argue that the more types of fees that are included in the QM rule's definition of points and fees, the more likely a mortgage is to breach the points and fees threshold and no longer qualify as a QM.[126] The definition of points and fees, therefore, may be important for determining whether a mortgage receives QM status, which can influence whether the lender will extend the loan.

The points and fees threshold varies based on the size of the loan. The threshold is higher for smaller loans because some fees are fixed costs that do not depend on the size of the loan. All else equal, smaller loans would be more likely to breach the thresholds unless their thresholds were higher. The thresholds, which are indexed for inflation, are currently as follows:

- 3% of the total loan amount for a loan greater than or equal to $100,000;
- $3,000 for a loan less than $100,000 but greater than or equal to $60,000;
- 5% of the total amount for a loan less than $60,000 but greater than or equal to $20,000;
- $1,000 for a loan less than $20,000 but greater than or equal to $12,500; and
- 8% of the total loan amount for a loan less than $12,500.[127]

A loan that is above the respective points and fees cap cannot be a QM.

The definition of points and fees includes certain costs associated with originating the mortgage. The term *point* refers to compensation paid up front to the lender by the borrower. A point is expressed as a percentage of the loan amount, with one point equal to 1% of the loan amount.[128] The definition of *fees* has several different categories of fees, but what is most pertinent with respect to H.R. 685 is that certain fees are excluded from the definition of points and fees if "the charge is paid to a third party unaffiliated with the creditor."[129] Certain fees paid to third parties affiliated[130] with the lender are included in the definition. H.R. 685 would change the treatment of fees for third parties affiliated with the lender by allowing (in some cases) those fees to also be excluded from the definition of points and fees. S. 1484 and S. 1910 would not exclude fees for third parties affiliated with the lender from the definition of points and fees, but would require a study that would examine the issue.

Policy Discussion

As mentioned above, the legislative proposals address the treatment of several types of fees. However, most of the policy debate surrounding fees for affiliated entities has focused on title insurance because title insurance is one of the larger fees associated with a mortgage that would be affected by the changes H.R. 685 proposes to the points and fees definition.[131] Title insurance involves "searching the property's records to ensure that [a particular individual is] the rightful owner and to check for liens."[132] Title insurance provides protection to the lender or borrower (depending on the type of policy) if there turns out to be a defect in the title. Under the current definition for points and fees, fees for title insurance provided by a title insurer that is independent of or unaffiliated with the lender may be *excluded* from the points and fees definition, but the fees for an affiliated title insurer must be *included* in the definition of points and fees. H.R. 685 would allow fees for affiliated title insurance to be treated the same as independent title insurance, and both would be excluded from the points and fees definition.

The cap on points and fees is intended to protect consumers from predatory loans by limiting fees that can be placed on a QM and by aligning the incentives of the lender and the borrower. Lenders can be compensated through points that are paid up front or through interest payments over the life of the loan. The method by which the lender receives compensation may influence the lender's incentive to evaluate the borrower's ability to repay the mortgage. As the CFPB notes in its preamble to the ATR rule, the cap on points and fees may make lenders "take more care in originating a loan when more of the return derives from performance over time (interest payments) rather [than] from upfront payments (points and fees). As such, this provision [the cap on points and fees] may offer lenders more incentive to underwrite these loans carefully."[133]

Supporters of H.R. 685 argue that expanding the definition of points and fees is important to ensuring that credit is available. The Mortgage Bankers Association, for example, stated that as a result of the current definition of points and fees, "many affiliated loans, particularly those made to low-and moderate-income borrowers, would not qualify as QMs and would be unlikely to be made or would only be available at higher rates due to heightened liability risks. Consumers would lose the ability to choose to take advantage of the convenience and market efficiencies offered by one-stop shopping."[134]

Putting the fees of affiliated and independent title insurers on equal footing in the points and fees definition, supporters argue, would enhance competition in the title insurance industry.[135]

Supporters also contend that because title insurance is regulated predominantly by the states and many states have policies in place to determine how title insurance is priced, there is less need to be concerned that title insurance fees are excessive.[136] They note that the Real Estate Settlement Procedures Act (RESPA)[137] allows affiliated business arrangements and already has protections in place for consumers, such as "a requirement to disclose affiliation to consumers."[138]

Opponents of H.R. 685 argue that, by narrowing the definition of points and fees to exclude affiliated providers, the bill "would allow lenders to increase the cost of loans and still be eligible for 'Qualified Mortgage' treatment. This revision risks eroding consumer protections and returning the mortgage market to the days of careless lending focused on short-term profits."[139] For this reason, the Obama Administration has said that "if the President were presented with H.R. 685, his senior advisors would recommend that he veto the bill."[140]

Critics also contend that removing affiliated title insurers from the points and fees definition would reduce the title insurance industry's incentive to make the price of title insurance, which some believe is already too high, "more reasonable."[141] They note that affiliated service providers are likely to be able to receive business through references from their affiliate and, therefore, "affiliates of a creditor may not have to compete in the market with other providers of a service and thus may charge higher prices that get passed on to the consumer."[142]

Escrow

H.R. 685, S. 1484, and S. 1910 would modify the definition of points and fees to exclude from the definition insurance held in escrow. Supporters of the proposals state that the bill would clarify that insurance held in escrow[143] should not be included in the definition of points and fees.[144] They argue that the drafting of the Dodd-Frank Act left unclear how insurance payments held in escrow should be treated in the definition. Opponents of the proposals have not cited this provision as a rationale for their opposition.

CBO estimates that H.R. 685 as ordered reported "would affect direct spending" but that "those effects would be insignificant."[145] The bill would not affect revenues or discretionary spending, according to CBO.

Rural Lending (H.R. 22, H.R. 1259 and S. 1484/S. 1910)[146]

Helping Expand Lending Practices in Rural Communities Act (H.R. 1259) was passed by the House on April 13, 2015. H.R. 1259 as passed would establish a temporary, two-year program in which individuals could petition the CFPB for counties that were not designated as rural by the CFPB to receive the rural designation. It also would establish evaluation criteria and an evaluation process for the CFPB to follow in assessing these petitions. A similar provision was included in the Fixing America's Surface Transportation Act (H.R. 22/P.L. 114-94). Section 103 of S. 1484 (Section 904 of S. 1910) would establish a petition process similar to the one proposed by H.R. 1259, but the process under S. 1484 and S. 1910 would not sunset after two years. The legislative proposals could increase the credit available to borrowers in rural areas but would reduce some of the protections put in place for rural consumers.

Definition of Rural

Statute allows for exemptions from certain consumer protection requirements for companies operating in rural areas. In implementing the requirements, the CFPB designates certain counties as rural. The exemptions and additional compliance options for lenders in rural areas stem from concerns that borrowers in these areas may have a harder time accessing credit than those in non-rural areas. For example, the ATR rule has an additional compliance option that allows small lenders operating in rural or underserved areas to originate balloon mortgages, subject to some restrictions.[147]

The Dodd-Frank Act specifies the additional compliance option for rural lenders, but it leaves the definition of rural to the discretion of the CFPB. Balloon mortgages originated by lenders in areas that are not designated as rural may be ineligible for the compliance option (although the CFPB has established a two-year transition period to allow "small"[148] lenders to originate balloon mortgages until January 2016, subject to some restrictions). Lenders that benefit from exemptions may offer products to their consumers that lenders in non-rural areas may be less likely to offer, but consumers in rural areas may not receive the same protections as those in non-rural areas.

When publishing the ATR rule, the CFPB stated that it considers its method of designating counties as rural, which is based on the U.S. Department of Agriculture's Urban Influence Codes,[149] to be consistent with the intent of the exemptions contained in statute. The CFPB estimated that its definition of rural results in 9.7% of the total U.S. population being in rural areas.[150] However, in light of various questions about its definition of rural raised during the comment period, the CFPB said in 2013 that it intended "to study whether the [definition] of 'rural' ... should be adjusted."[151] As a result, the CFPB issued a rule in September 2015 to expand the definition of rural as a means of facilitating access to credit in rural areas.[152] The new definition would have two prongs: an area could be deemed rural under the existing methodology involving the Urban Influence Codes or, if it is not designated as rural by that test, it could qualify under an alternative method that involves the Census Bureau's census block data.

To qualify for some of the exemptions, a lender not only must operate in a rural area but also must meet the CFPB's definition of small, which the CFPB also expanded in its September 2015 rule. Based on 2013 data, the CFPB estimates "that the number of rural small creditors would increase from about 2,400 to about 4,100."[153]

Policy Discussion

Although rule is intended to expand credit availability, the CFPB notes that its analysis "did not find specific evidence that the final provisions would increase access to credit."[154] The CFPB explains that its inability to estimate the change in credit availability from the rule may be due to data limitations that prevent it from testing certain hypotheses.[155] Alternatively, the CFPB notes that the change in credit availability may be difficult to estimate because borrowers in rural areas already may be adequately served by lenders and therefore may not benefit from the CFPB's expanded definition.[156]

The CFPB maintains that the use of census blocks, as suggested in its rule, allows for a more granular approach, but critics have argued that the new approach "is still inadequate because census tracts are only updated once every 10 years."[157] Supporters of the proposals contend the CFPB's method of designating counties as rural is inflexible and may not account for "atypical population distributions or geographic boundaries."[158] The proposals are intended, supporters argue, to provide a way to challenge a CFPB designation and invites individuals "to participate in their government and provide input on matters of local knowledge. It is about making the Federal Government more accessible, more accountable, and more responsive to the people who know their local communities best."[159]

CBO estimates that H.R. 1259 as ordered reported would increase direct spending by $1 million over the next 10 years but would not affect revenues or discretionary spending.[160]

Mortgage Escrow and Servicing (H.R. 1529)[161]

The Community Institution Mortgage Relief Act of 2015 (H.R. 1529) was reported by the House Committee on Financial Services on April 6, 2015.[162] H.R. 1529 as reported would make two modifications to CFPB mortgage rules. It would (1) exempt from certain escrow requirements any mortgage held by a lender with assets of $10 billion or less if the mortgage is held in the lender's portfolio for three years and (2) exempt from certain servicing requirements any servicer that annually services 20,000 mortgages or fewer. Supporters of H.R. 1529 argue that the bill would reduce the burden on small lenders and servicers of complying with these regulations while giving added flexibility to consumers. Opponents argue that the bill would roll back consumer protections that were put in place in response to the housing and foreclosure crisis.

Escrow Accounts

An *escrow* account is an account that a "mortgage lender may set up to pay certain recurring property-related expenses ... such as property taxes and homeowner's insurance."[163] Property taxes and homeowner's insurance often are lump-sum payments owed annually or semiannually. To ensure a borrower has enough money to make these payments, a lender may divide up the amount owed and add it to a borrower's monthly payment. The additional amount paid each month is placed in the escrow account and then drawn on by the mortgage servicer that administers the account to make the required annual or semiannual payments. Maintaining escrow accounts for borrowers is an additional cost to banks and may be especially costly for smaller firms.

An escrow account is not required for all types of mortgages but had been required for at least one year for higher-priced mortgage loans even before the Dodd-Frank Act.[164] A *higher-priced mortgage loan* is a loan with an APR "that exceeds an 'average prime offer rate'[165] for a comparable transaction by 1.5 or more percentage points for transactions secured by a first lien, or by 3.5 or more percentage points for transactions secured by a subordinate lien."[166] If the first lien is a *jumbo mortgage* (above the conforming loan limit[167] for Fannie Mae and Freddie Mac), then it is considered a higher-priced mortgage loan if its APR is 2.5 percentage points or more above the average prime offer rate. The Dodd-Frank Act, among other things, extended the amount of time an escrow account for a higher-priced mortgage loan must be maintained from one year to five years, although the escrow account can be terminated after five years only if certain conditions are met. It also provided additional disclosure requirements.[168]

The Dodd-Frank Act gave the CFPB the discretion to exempt from certain escrow requirements lenders operating predominantly in rural areas if the lenders satisfied certain conditions.[169] The CFPB's escrow rule included exemptions from escrow requirements for lenders that (1) operate predominantly in rural or underserved areas; (2) extend 2,000 mortgages or fewer; (3) have less than $2 billion in total assets; and (4) do not escrow for any mortgage they service (with some exceptions).[170] Additionally, a lender that satisfies the above criteria must intend to hold the loan in its portfolio to be exempt from the escrow requirement for that loan. H.R. 1529 would expand the exemption such that a lender also would be exempt from maintaining an escrow account for a mortgage as long as it satisfied two criteria: (1) the mortgage is held by the lender in its portfolio for three or more years and (2) the lender has $10 billion or less in assets.

Policy Discussion

When the CFPB issued its escrow rule in January 2013, it estimated that "there are 2,612 exempt creditors who originated ... first-lien higher-priced mortgage loans in 2011."[171] It also estimated that there would be 5,087 lenders with $10 billion or less in total assets who, collectively, originated 91,142 first-lien higher-priced mortgage loans in 2011 that would *not* be exempt from the escrow requirements.[172] If H.R. 1529 had been in place in 2011, those additional 5,087 lenders would have been exempt from the escrow requirements for the loans held in portfolio for three or more years.[173]

Supporters of H.R. 1529 argue that expanding the escrow exemption is important for reducing the regulatory burden on small banks. Small banks already would have the incentive, the argument goes, to make sure the borrower will pay taxes and insurance even without the escrow account because the lender is exposed to some of the risk by keeping the mortgage in its portfolio.[174] Because of this "skin in the game," supporters argue the escrow requirement is unduly burdensome for small banks. They also believe the requirement can be an unnecessary burden to consumers who would rather manage their taxes and insurance payments on their own, especially if those consumers have a history of making their required payments on previous loans.[175]

Opponents of H.R. 1529 argue that the escrow requirement is an important consumer protection. The escrow account is required for higher-priced mortgage loans, and critics contend that the higher interest rate on those loans reflects the fact that borrowers with these loans often are riskier subprime borrowers.[176] Because these borrowers already face a higher risk of default, opponents of H.R. 1529 argue the escrow requirement is important for ensuring these borrowers are not, in the words of Ranking Member Waters, "being blindsided by additional costs at the end of each year."[177] They argue that the exemption the CFPB gave for certain smaller entities already strikes the appropriate balance between reducing the regulatory burden for some banks and protecting consumers.

Mortgage Servicers

The second part of H.R. 1529 addresses *mortgage servicers*. Servicers received added attention from Congress after the surge in foreclosures following the bursting of the housing bubble. The Dodd-Frank Act imposed additional requirements on servicers to protect borrowers through amendments to TILA and RESPA.[178] The new servicing protections[179] include, among other things, additional disclosure requirements about the timing of rate changes, requirements for how payments would be credited, obligations to address errors in a timely fashion, and guidance on when foreclosure could be initiated and how servicers must have continuity of contact with borrowers. The CFPB issued rules implementing those changes.[180]

Servicers that service 5,000 mortgages or fewer and only service mortgages that they or an affiliate owns or originated are considered *small servicers* and are exempted from some but not all TILA and RESPA servicing requirements.[181] H.R. 1529 would modify the exemption for the rules implemented under RESPA by directing the CFPB to provide exemptions to or adjustments from the RESPA servicing provisions for servicers that service 20,000 mortgages or fewer "in order to reduce regulatory burdens while appropriately balancing consumer protections."[182] The RESPA servicing provisions that could be affected by H.R. 1529 include, among other things, how escrow accounts (if they are required) would be administered, disclosure to an applicant about whether his or her servicing can be sold or transferred, notice to the borrower if the loan is transferred, prohibitions on the servicer relating to fees and imposing certain types of insurance, and other consumer protections.[183]

Policy Discussion

In its discussion of its servicing rule, the CFPB notes that "servicers that service relatively few loans, all of which they either originated or hold on portfolio, generally have incentives to service well."[184] The incentive to service the loans well comes from the fact that "foregoing the returns to scale of a large servicing portfolio indicates that the servicer chooses not to profit from volume, and owning or having originated all of the loans serviced indicates a stake in either the performance of the loan or in an ongoing relationship with the borrower."[185] The CFPB, therefore, found that an "exemption may be appropriate only for servicers that service a relatively small number of loans and either own or originated the loans they service."[186]

The CFPB set the loan threshold at 5,000 loans because it concluded that this category "identifies the group of servicers that make loans only or largely in their local communities or more generally have incentives to provide high levels of customer contact and information."[187] The CFPB's data analysis of the threshold concluded that

> With the threshold set at 5,000 loans, the Bureau estimates that over 98% of insured depositories and credit unions with under $2 billion in assets fall beneath the threshold. In contrast, only 29% of such institutions with over $2 billion in assets fall beneath the threshold and only 11% of such institutions with over $10 billion in assets do so. Further, over 99.5% of insured depositories and credit unions that meet the traditional threshold for a community bank—$1 billion in assets—fall beneath the threshold. The Bureau estimates there are about 60 million closed-end mortgage loans overall, with about 5.7 million serviced by insured depositories and credit unions that qualify for the exemption.[188]

The CFPB's 2013 rulemaking did not discuss the effect of setting the threshold at 20,000 loans, as H.R. 1529 would, but it noted that if "the loan count threshold were set at 10,000 mortgage loans, for example, over 99.5% of insured depositories and credit unions with under $2 billion in assets would fall beneath the threshold. However, 50% of insured depositories with over $2 billion in assets and 20% of those with over $10 billion in assets would fall beneath the threshold."[189] Those entities that service more than 5,000 loans, the CFPB contends, may be more likely to use a different servicing model that would not have the same "incentives to provide high levels of customer contact and information."[190] The CFPB, therefore, set the threshold at 5,000 loans.

Supporters of H.R. 1529 argue that the bill is intended to give the CFPB the discretion to either provide "exemptions or adjustments to the requirements of the existing codes section and should do so appropriately balancing consumer protections. So the near-small institutions will either get the relief currently granted to the small institutions or a bit less relief, and that will be determined by the CFPB."[191] Raising the threshold from 5,000 loans to 20,000 loans, supporters argue, "will better delineate small servicers from the large servicers, and give credit union and community banks greater flexibility to ensure that more of their customers can stay in their homes."[192]

Opponents of H.R. 1529 have contended that the exemptions in the CFPB's regulations are sufficient to protect small lenders and that expanding the exemptions would weaken the protections available to consumers. They note that by not only raising the threshold but also removing the requirement that servicers own the mortgage, the servicers would have "less skin in that game if bad servicing practices were to result in default and foreclosure."[193] Critics point to mortgage servicers in particular as actors that performed poorly during the foreclosure crisis and should not receive additional exemptions from CFPB regulations.[194]

CBO estimates that H.R. 1529 as ordered reported would "increase direct spending by less than $500,000 for expenses of the CFPB to prepare and enforce new rules" but would not affect revenues or discretionary spending.[195]

Portfolio Qualified Mortgage (H.R. 1210 and S. 1484/S. 1910)[196]

The Portfolio Lending and Mortgage Access Act (H.R. 1210) was passed by the House on November 18, 2015. H.R. 1210 would establish a new qualified mortgage (QM) category for a mortgage held in a lender's portfolio. Section 106 of S. 1484 (Section 907 of S. 1910) would also establish a portfolio QM category. S. 1484/S. 1910 would require a loan to meet stricter criteria than under H.R. 1210 but would have more relaxed portfolio requirements than H.R. 1210. The legislative proposals are intended to increase credit availability and to reduce the regulatory burden on lenders. Critics argue that the proposals would go too far in reducing consumer protections and would allow lenders to receive legal protections for offering risky, non-standard mortgage products.

The Ability-to-Repay Rule and Portfolio Loans

Title XIV of the Dodd-Frank Act established the ability-to-repay (ATR) requirement. Under the ATR requirement, a lender must determine based on documented and verified information that, at the time a mortgage loan is made, the borrower has the ability to repay the loan. The rule enumerates the type of information that a lender must consider and verify prior to originating a loan, including the applicant's income or assets, credit history, outstanding debts, and other criteria. Lenders that fail to comply with the ATR rule could be subject to legal liability could be subject to legal liability, such as the payment of certain statutory damages.[197]

A lender can comply with the ATR rule in one of two ways. A lender can either originate a mortgage that meets the less concrete underwriting and product feature standards of the General ATR Option or a mortgage that satisfies the more stringent, specific standards of the Qualified Mortgage. A QM is a mortgage that satisfies certain underwriting and product feature requirements. There are several different types of QM, with the different categories applying to different lenders and having different underwriting and product feature requirements. For example, the Standard QM that is available to all lenders requires the mortgage to not have balloon payments or a loan term over 30 years, has restrictions on the fees that can be charged, and has other requirements that must be met in order for the mortgage to receive QM status. These underwriting and product feature requirements are intended to ensure that a mortgage receiving QM status satisfies certain minimum standards, with the standards intended to offer protections to borrowers. A loan that satisfies the less concrete standards of the General ATR Option, in contrast, is allowed to have a balloon payment and a term in excess of 30 years so long as the lender verifies that the borrower would have the ability to repay the loan.

If a lender originates a mortgage that receives QM status, then it is presumed to have complied with the ATR rule and receives legal protections that could reduce its potential legal liability.[198] As mentioned above, a lender can comply with the ATR rule by making a mortgage that is not a QM and instead satisfies the General ATR Option, but the lender will not receive the additional legal protections. The definition of a QM, therefore, is important to a lender seeking to minimize its *legal risk*. Because of this legal risk, some are concerned that, at least in the short term, few mortgages will be originated that do not meet the QM standards due to the legal protections that QMs afford lenders, even though there are other means of complying with the ATR rule.[199]

If a mortgage does not receive QM status under the Standard QM – the general approach that most focus on when discussing the QM compliance options – the mortgage may still receive QM status if it complies with the Small Creditor Portfolio QM option. To do so, three broad sets of criteria must be satisfied. First, the loan must be held in portfolio for at least three years (subject to several exceptions).[200] Second, the loan must be held by a small lender, which is defined as a lender who originated 2,000 or fewer mortgages in the previous year and has less than $2 billion in assets.[201] Third, the loan must meet certain underwriting and product feature requirements.[202]

Compared to the Standard QM, the Small Creditor Portfolio QM has less prescriptive underwriting requirements. For example, to receive QM status under the Standard QM, a borrower must have a debt-to-income (DTI) ratio below 43% after accounting for the payments associated with the mortgage and other debt obligations, but under the Small Creditor Portfolio QM, the lender is required to consider and verify the borrower's DTI but does not have a specific threshold that the borrower must be below.

The CFPB was willing to relax the underwriting standards for some portfolio loans because it believed "that portfolio loans made by small creditors are particularly likely to be made responsibly and to be affordable for the consumer."[203] By keeping the loan in portfolio, the CFPB argues, small creditors have added incentive to consider whether the borrower will be able to repay the loan[204] because the lender retains the default risk and could be exposed to losses if the borrower does not repay. This exposure, the argument goes, would encourage small creditors to provide additional scrutiny during the underwriting process, even in the absence of a legal requirement to do so. Keeping the mortgage in portfolio is intended to align "consumers' and creditors' interests regarding ability to repay."[205]

Policy Discussion

The Small Creditor Portfolio QM is intended to increase the amount of credit that is available to consumers by making it easier for small lenders to extend portfolio loans. Some in Congress argue that the Small Creditor Portfolio QM, while useful to expand credit and reduce regulatory burden, is too narrow. They propose establishing an additional portfolio QM option that would have more relaxed eligibility criteria. The proposals would allow larger lenders to participate and would not require all of the Small Creditor Portfolio QM's underwriting and product feature requirements (such as the DTI ratio) to be met in order to receive QM status.

Supporters of an expanded portfolio lending option argue that when a larger lender holds the mortgage in portfolio, it too has the incentive to ensure that the borrower will repay the loan because it is also exposed to the risk of default. They argue that this incentive is present whether the lender is large or small. The incentive to ensure the loan is properly underwritten, supporters argue, is sufficient to merit the loan receiving QM status and the commensurate legal protections. Extending the legal protections to portfolio loans, the argument goes, will encourage lenders to expand credit and allow more individuals to purchase homes.

Critics of the proposals contend that the incentive alignment associated with holding a mortgage in portfolio is not sufficient to justify extending QM status to portfolio loans held by large lenders. Certain traits that are more likely to be found in small lenders, they argue, are also important for ensuring that a lender thoroughly evaluates a borrower's ability to repay. The CFPB limited the Small Creditor Portfolio QM to small lenders because the CFPB believes the "relationship-based" business model often employed by small lenders may make small lenders better able to assess a borrower's ability to repay than larger lenders.[206] Additionally, the CFPB argues that small lenders often have close ties to their communities, which provides added incentive to thoroughly underwrite their mortgages for the borrower's ability to repay.[207] The level at which a lender should not be considered small because it no longer is influenced by its ties to its communities, however, is subject to much debate.

CBO estimates that H.R. 1210 as ordered reported could affect direct spending but that the effect would be insignificant.[208] The bill would not affect revenues. CBO notes that the more relaxed definition of QM could result in higher losses to financial institutions which could increase their likelihood of failure and potential cost to the government, but CBO states that this is a small probability that "CBO's baseline estimates would result in additional costs to the federal government of less than $500,000 over the 2016-2025 period."[209]

Integrated Disclosure Forms (H.R. 3192 and S. 1484/S. 1910)[210]

The Homebuyers Assistance Act (H.R. 3192) was passed by the House on October 7, 2015. H.R. 3192 as passed would prevent the TILA and RESPA integrated disclosure requirements from being enforced until February 1, 2016. It would also prohibit anyone from filing a suit against a lender related to the TILA-RESPA integrated disclosure forms during that time period so long as the lender has made a good faith effort to comply with the requirements.

Section 117 of S. 1484 (Section 918 of S. 1910) would provide a safe harbor for lenders related to the integrated disclosure forms. It would make a lender that provides the required disclosures not "subject to any civil, criminal, or administrative action or penalty for failure to fully comply".[211] The safe harbor would be in effect until one month after the CFPB director certifies that the new disclosures "are accurate and in compliance with all State laws".[212] In addition, S. 1484/S. 1910 would eliminate the requirement that a mortgage closing be delayed three days if the lender offered the borrower a mortgage with a lower annual percentage rate than the rate that was originally offered.

Integrated Disclosures

On November 20, 2013, the CFPB issued the TILA-RESPA Final Rule that would require mortgage lenders to use more easily understood and streamlined mortgage disclosure forms.[213] TILA and RESPA have long required lenders to provide consumers disclosures about the estimated and actual real estate settlement costs and financial terms of the mortgages they offer. These disclosures are intended to help consumers compare the terms and make informed decisions regarding the suitability of various mortgage products and services they are offered. However, TILA and RESPA required disclosures of duplicative information while using inconsistent language, which might have led to increased regulatory costs and consumer confusion.[214] In light of these concerns, Sections 1098 and 1100A of the Dodd-Frank Act required the CFPB to develop "a single, integrated disclosure for mortgage loan transactions ... to aid the borrower ... in understanding the transaction by utilizing readily understandable language to simplify the technical nature of the disclosures" that remains compliant with both TILA and RESPA.[215]

The TILA-RESPA Final Rule is the culmination of more than two years of study through, among other things, consumer testing and a Small Business Review Panel.[216] The Board of Governors of the Federal Reserve System and the Department of Housing and Urban Development, which prior to the Dodd-Frank Act implemented TILA and RESPA, had attempted but failed to make similar changes to these disclosure forms. In short, combining these mortgage disclosures into a single form was a massive undertaking, and, upon taking effect, the TILA-RESPA Final Rule will have a significant impact on consumers, lenders, and other participants in the mortgage market.

Policy Discussion

The CFPB chose to give the industry until August 1, 2015—nearly two years from the date on which the Final Rule was first publicly released—to comply. In spite of this lead-time, mortgage bankers and lenders in recent months have expressed concern about their inability to update software and make other necessary changes to meet the compliance deadline.[217] This led some to ask CFPB Director Richard Cordray for additional time to comply before the CFPB starts enforcing the law.[218] Those requests went unheeded until it was discovered that, because of an "administrative error,"[219] the August

1st effective date would violate a provision of the Congressional Review Act[220] that prevents a *major rule*[221] from going into effect until at least 60 days from the date on which the rule was published in the *Federal Register* or was formally reported to Congress, whichever is later. The CFPB recently announced that,"[t]o comply with the CRA and to help ensure the smooth implementation of the TILA-RESPA Final Rule, the Bureau is extending the effective date ... [from August 1 to] October 3, 2015.... "[222]

The CFPB has also announced what some have characterized as a restrained enforcement period related to the integrated disclosures.[223] In a letter to Members of Congress, the CFPB stated that its "oversight of the implementation of the Rule will be sensitive to the progress made by those entities that have squarely focused on making good-faith efforts to come into compliance with the Rule on time."[224] The CFPB also announced that it sent a letter to industry trade groups in which it stated that

> During initial examinations for compliance with the rule, the Bureau's examiners will evaluate an institution's compliance management system and overall efforts to come into compliance, recognizing the scope and scale of changes necessary for each supervised institution to achieve effective compliance. Examiners will expect supervised entities to make good faith efforts to comply with the rule's requirements in a timely manner. Specifically, examiners will consider: the institution's implementation plan, including actions taken to update policies, procedures, and processes; its training of appropriate staff; and, its handling of early technical problems or other implementation challenges.[225]

Supporters of H.R. 3192 and S. 1484/S. 1910 argue that an additional two months is insufficient for lenders to make the upgrades needed to satisfy the deadline and that the restrained enforcement period does not address several underlying concerns. Supporters of a safe harbor contend that lenders should have to use the new disclosure forms and procedures but should have a grace period to test out the new systems.[226] The grace period that supporters are seeking would not just apply to actions taken by the regulators but would also protect lenders from being sued by borrowers claiming that the correct disclosure forms and procedures were not followed. The threat of this private litigation risk, supporters argue, is not addressed by the CFPB's extension and could cause some lenders to delay or cancel mortgage closings if there is uncertainty about how the new process should be implemented.[227] In addition, supporters of a delay argue that there is uncertainty as to whether the rule conflicts with state law, and the potential conflicts should be clarified prior to implementation.[228]

Critics of delaying the implementation argue that the actions already taken by the CFPB are sufficient to protect lenders from the risks that they face and that the extended implementation timeframe allows lenders enough time to adopt the necessary systems and processes. They also argue "that private liability works to ensure that regulated entities are diligent in complying promptly with the new TRID disclosures" and that the private liability should not be delayed.[229] Critics also note that the litigation risk "that [is] part of the new TRID rule has been overstated, as private litigants rarely bring actions that prevail under the provisions of TILA that are implicated by the new TRID disclosures."[230] The delay that some are hoping for, according to critics, "is unnecessary in light of the limited liability for disclosure- related violations under TILA and the steps already taken by the CFPB."[231] If a further delay was put in place, some argue that homeowners "who would receive false or misleading mortgage cost disclosures during such a period would have no remedy."[232]

CBO estimates that H.R. 3192 as ordered reported would result in an increase in direct spending that would be negligible.[233] The bill would not affect revenues or discretionary spending.

Privacy Notifications (H.R. 22, H.R. 601, and S. 1484/S. 1910)[234]

The Eliminate Privacy Notice Confusion Act (H.R. 601) was passed by the House on April 13, 2015. It was then included in the Fixing America's Surface Transportation Act (H.R. 22/P.L. 114 94). Section 101 of S. 1484 (Section 902 of S. 1910) includes similar language. These proposals would reduce the number of scenarios under which financial firms were required to send customers privacy notices. Under H.R. 601, financial firms would no longer be required to send annual privacy notices if their privacy policy had not changed. Under S. 1484/S. 1910, financial firms would no longer be required to send annual privacy notices if their privacy policy had not changed and if the firm made the most recent privacy notice available to customers electronically. Cases in which third-party information sharing triggers notification and the opportunity to opt out under current law would remain unchanged.[235] It is an example of a regulatory relief bill amending a law that predates the financial crisis.

Background

Under a provision of the Gramm-Leach-Bliley Act (15 U.S.C. §6803), financial firms, including banks, are required to send customers privacy notices when they establish a relationship with the customer and annually thereafter. Firms also are required to send customers notices explaining how customers may opt out of allowing the firm to share their personal information with third parties, under certain circumstances.[236]

Policy Discussion

Financial firms argue that the privacy notice requirement is unduly burdensome to them and of little value to customers because the notices are lengthy, confusing, and thus likely to be ignored. Defenders of current law argue that it provides consumer protection and safeguards privacy.[237]

The CFPB contends that a rule it issued in 2014 modifying Regulation P (which implements 15 U.S.C. §6803) will reduce the regulatory burden of compliance without undermining the policy's benefits.[238] The 2014 CFPB rule allows firms under certain conditions to post privacy notices on the Internet rather than mail hard copies to customers. The rule requires firms to continue sending printed notices when privacy policies are changed or information is shared with third parties. Firms are required to provide annual notification that privacy notices are available on the Internet and to provide printed notices upon request. Some believe additional relief is needed beyond what was provided in the 2014 CFPB rule.

CBO estimates that H.R. 601 as ordered reported would result in an increase in direct spending that would not be significant.[239] The bill would not affect revenues or discretionary spending.

SUPERVISION AND ENFORCEMENT

Supervision refers to the power to examine banks, instruct banks to modify their behavior, and to impose reporting requirements on banks to ensure compliance with rules. In some cases, examiners confirm whether banks meet quantitative targets and thresholds set by regulation; in others, they have discretion to interpret whether a bank's actions satisfy the goals of a regulation. Enforcement is the authority to take certain legal actions, such as imposing fines, against an institution that fails to comply with rules and laws.

While regulators generally view their supervisory and enforcement actions as striking the appropriate balance between ensuring that institutions are well managed and minimizing the burden facing banks, others believe the regulators are overreaching and preventing banks from serving their customers.

Bank Exams

On-site examinations, which stem from a regulator's visitorial powers, are part of the supervisory process. A regulator's visitorial powers include

> (i) Examination of a bank; (ii) Inspection of a bank's books and records; (iii) Regulation and supervision of activities authorized or permitted pursuant to federal banking law; and (iv) Enforcing compliance with any applicable Federal or state laws concerning those activities, including through investigations that seek to ascertain compliance through production of non-public information by the bank... [with certain limitations].[240]

Exam Frequency for Small Banks (H.R. 22, H.R. 1553 and S. 1484/S. 1910)[241]

Section 109 of S. 1484 (Section 910 of S. 1910) would raise the size thresholds for banks subject to an 18-month exam cycle from $500 million to $1 billion in assets if the bank received an outstanding exam rating. For banks that received a good exam rating, it gives the regulator discretion to raise the threshold from $100 million up to $1 billion (currently, the regulator may raise it to up to $500 million) in assets if it believes raising it would be consistent with safety and soundness.

H.R. 1553 was passed by the House on October 6, 2015. It was then included in the Fixing America's Surface Transportation Act (H.R. 22/P.L. 114-94). It would raise the size thresholds for banks subject to an 18-month exam cycle from $500 million to $1 billion in assets if the bank received an outstanding exam rating and from $100 million to $200 million if the bank received a good exam rating. It gives the bank regulator discretion to raise the latter threshold from $200 million up to $1 billion (currently, the regulator may raise it to up to $500 million) in assets if it believes raising it would be consistent with safety and soundness. CBO estimates that the net budgetary effects of the bill would be insignificant.[242]

Background

Regulators examine banks at least once every 12 months, but banks with less than $500 million in total assets that have high supervisory ratings and meet certain conditions are examined once every 18 months.[243] Regulators changed the frequency of examinations in 2007 from once every 12 months to once every 18 months pursuant to the Financial Services Regulatory Relief Act.[244] In contrast, some large and complex banks have examiners conducting full-time monitoring on-site. The bank receives a report of the findings when an examination is completed.

Policy Discussion

CBO estimates that 500 to 600 institutions would see the frequency of their exams reduced under H.R. 1553.[245] Regulators have taken steps to reduce the regulatory burden associated with on-site examinations. The Fed introduced a new examination program in January 2014 that, according to Governor Tarullo, "more explicitly links examination intensity to the individual community bank's risk profile.... The new program calls for examiners to spend less time on low-risk compliance issues at community banks."[246] In testimony before the Senate Banking Committee, Governor Tarullo also stated,

> Recognizing the burden that the on-site presence of many examiners can place on the day-to-day business of a community bank, we are also working to increase our level of off-site supervisory activities.... To that end, last year we completed a pilot on conducting parts of the labor-intensive loan review off-site using electronic records from banks.[247]

Although regulators have already taken these steps to reduce regulatory burden related to exams, the OCC has proposed increasing the threshold for the 18-month exam cycle to banks with $750 million.[248]

In response to a congressional request, bank regulators' inspectors general conducted studies on the regulatory burden to small banks stemming from compliance with supervisory exams. From 2007 to 2011, OCC community bank exams typically took 120 days or less (as they are intended to), but sometimes took up to a year, and occasionally took over a year.[249] The length of exams was slightly longer from 2008 to 2010, when the most banks were failing. In 2011, FDIC community bank risk-management exams varied in length from an average of 335 hours to 1,820 hours based on the size of the bank and its supervisory rating. From 2007 to 2011, exams of banks with poor supervisory ratings became shorter over time and banks with good supervisory ratings took longer over time. In addition, the FDIC conducts thousands of compliance and a few CRA exams annually. In 2011, the FDIC spent an average of 24 days to 57 days on-site for risk management exams, based on supervisory rating.[250] Fed exams (not including state-led exams, which took longer), averaged 63 days to 79 days between 2007 and 2011, peaking in 2009.[251] Although costs cannot be derived directly from hours spent on exams, this data may nevertheless give some indication of regulatory burden caused by meeting with examination staff and uncertainty created while waiting for exam results.

One concern raised by small banks is that there are economies of scale in compliance—in other words, compliance costs rise less than proportionately with size. The FDIC inspector general's study provides some evidence of economies of scale in compliance in the area of exams. It found that exams of banks with less than $50 million in assets averaged 335 hours, whereas banks with $500 million-$1 billion in assets averaged 850 hours in 2011. In other words, exams for larger banks took longer, but the increase in hours was not linear with the increase in assets.[252]

Exam Ombudsman and Appeals Process (H.R. 1941 and S. 1484/S. 1910)[253]

H.R. 1941 was ordered to be reported by the House Financial Services Committee on July 29, 2015. It would require regulators to provide a bank a final exam report within 60 days of the conclusion the exam exit interview or when follow up materials have been provided. It would require the exit interview to take place no more than nine months after the exam begins unless the agency provides written notice for an extension. It sets detailed exam standards for commercial loans to prevent an adverse action when the underlying collateral has deteriorated. It would require the banking regulators to harmonize their standards for non-accrual loans. It would establish an ombudsman (called the Office of Independent Examination Review) within the Federal Financial Institutions Examination Council (FFIEC)[254] to investigate complaints from banks about supervisory exams. The head of the office would be appointed by FFIEC. It would prohibit specific actions by the supervisor in retaliation for appealing. It would give banks the right to appeal exam results to the ombudsman or an administrative law judge, and would not allow the ombudsman or judge to defer to the supervisor's opinions. It would not permit further appeal by the supervisor, but would allow the bank to appeal this decision to appellate court. It would add the CFPB to the statutory appeals process,[255] including the new ombudsman.

Similarly, section 104 of S. 1484 (Section 905 of S. 1910) would establish an ombudsman (called the Office of Independent Examination Review) within FFIEC to investigate complaints from banks about supervisory exams. The head of the office would be appointed by FFIEC to a five-year term, but could be removed by the President without cause. It would prohibit specific actions by the supervisor in retaliation for appealing. It would add the CFPB to the statutory appeals process, including the new ombudsman.

Background

Bank regulators have established multiple processes for a bank to appeal the results of its examination.[256] Regulators typically encourage a bank to attempt to resolve any dispute informally through discussions with the bank examiner.[257] The Riegle Community Development and Regulatory Improvement Act of 1994[258] required banking regulators to establish a formal independent appeals process for supervisory findings, appoint an independent ombudsman, and create safeguards to prevent retaliation (which is not defined in the act) against a bank that disputes their examination findings.[259] While each ombudsman's exact role varies by agency, they generally fit the description of the Fed's—to "serve as a facilitator and mediator for the timely resolution of complaints."[260] The independent appeals process currently involves bank examiners at the agency that were not involved in the examination, as well as agency leadership. Only the OCC allows banks to appeal an examination directly to the agency's ombudsman.[261]

Policy Discussion

By statute,[262] banks may already appeal exam results to the regulator that conducted it, and each banking agency already has an ombudsman. Skeptics view the creation of an additional ombudsman for all banking agencies as redundant. Proponents of the legislation argue that the proposed ombudsman would be more independent from the banking agencies, although it would be funded by the agencies[263] and would still be located within a forum (FFIEC) controlled by the banking agencies. The role of ombudsman in the appeals process in H.R. 1491 would be new for all of the regulators except the OCC, however.

In exams, supervisors are balancing the profitability of the bank with the risk of bank failure to the taxpayer. Critics of H.R. 1941 argue that shifting the appeals process away from the regulator to the newly created ombudsman would put the taxpayer at risk by making it more likely that supervisory decisions would be overturned. Further, the new ombudsman would arguably not have "inside knowledge" of the supervisory process, which involves discretion. Proponents of H.R. 1491 argue that in the current appeals process, the supervisor plays the role of prosecutor, judge, and jury, and therefore the supervisor is unlikely to be willing to admit that a mistake had been made in the original exam. In the American Bankers Association's view, the current process is "time-consuming, expensive, and rarely result in a reversal of the matter being appealed. There also is a concern among ABA members that appealing will risk examiner retribution,"[264] though retaliation is already forbidden by statute. The knowledge that exams could be independently appealed could make examiners more careful to adhere to guidelines, or it could make them less willing to make adverse decisions so as to avoid the "hassle" of appeals.

The urgency of changing the appeals process depends on how well it is currently working. Since all supervisory information is confidential, disputes about the fairness of exams and appeals is prone to a "he said/she said" dynamic between bank and regulator that is difficult for a third party to evaluate. The frequency of appeals might give some indication of bank displeasure with the examination process. In response to a congressional request, bank regulators' inspectors general conducted studies on the regulatory burden to small banks and found that banks only formally appealed 22 OCC exam results (informally appealed 24 more), 23 FDIC exams (informally appealed 18 more), and 12 Fed exams (no informal appeal data) out of the thousands of exams performed between 2007 and 2011.[265] However, banks might not appeal an exam result they thought was unfair if they thought their appeal had no chance of succeeding. Further, many disputes are resolved informally through the supervisory process, before an exam is completed.

Call Report Reform (S. 1484/S. 1910)[266]

The primary source of bank regulatory data is the quarterly Reports of Condition and Income, or call report, that a bank submits to its regulator. Section 119 of S. 1484 (Section 920 of S. 1910) requires the banking regulators to review the current call report and, "to the extent appropriate," develop a shorter call report.

Background

Bank supervision is not a one-time event that occurs when the examiner visits the bank, but rather is an ongoing process that includes monitoring data collected from banks. A primary source of data is the call report, in which banks report data on various aspects of their operations using a standard definition so that data can be compared across banks by the regulators and the public.[267] The call report is made up of various schedules, each with multiple line items, and the number of schedules and items that a bank must report depends on its size and activities.

Current statute requires the regulators to review call reports every five years in order to eliminate any information or schedule that "is no longer necessary or appropriate."[268] This requirement does not reference the size of the institution. The next review is due by October 13, 2016. FFIEC has announced that they are accelerating this review and expect it to take effect for the December 2015 or March 2016 call reports.[269] The bank regulators released a proposed rule in September 2015 that proposes to delete a number of items from current call reports, exempt banks with under $1 billion in assets from four items, surveys regulators to find out the usefulness of each item on the call report, and dialogues with banks to find out the regulatory burden associated with reporting each item, among other things.[270] They are also "evaluating the feasibility and merits of creating a streamlined version of the quarterly Call Report for community institutions...."[271]

Statute also required the regulators to modernize the call report process in 1994 and 2000. Included was a requirement that the regulators eliminate call report items that were "not warranted for reasons of safety and soundness or other public purposes."[272]

Policy Discussion

The FDIC has argued that call reports "provide an early indication that an institution's risk profile may be changing" and are therefore important parts of the supervision process.[273] Removing too many items from the call report could mute the early warning signal it provides. Proponents of the legislation argue that call reports are currently unduly complex and burdensome for community banks with traditional business operations. The call report is currently structured to lower the burden on small banks relative to larger and more complex banks, however. The FDIC states that

> The Call Report itself is tiered to size and complexity of the filing institution, in that more than one-third of the data items are linked to asset

> size or activity levels. Based on this tiering alone, community banks never, or rarely, need to fill out a number of pages in the Call Report, not counting the data items and pages that are not applicable to a particular bank based on its business model. For example, a typical $75 million community bank showed reportable amounts in only 14 percent of the data items in the Call Report and provided data on 40 pages. Even a relatively large community bank, at $1.3 billion, showed reportable amounts in only 21 percent of data items and provided data on 47 pages.[274]

There is no official data on the regulatory burden associated with call reports. As evidence that the regulatory burden has increased over time, the American Bankers Association claims that the number of items required in call reports has increased from 309 in 1980 to 1,955 in 2012.[275] The Independent Community Bankers of America, a trade association representing community banks, conducted a survey which found that "[a]lmost three quarters of respondents stated that the number of hours required to complete the call report had increased over the last ten years. Over one third of respondents indicated a significant increase in hours over this period. Well over three quarters of respondents noted increased costs in call report preparation with almost one third noting that costs increased significantly."[276] The survey showed mixed evidence of economies of scale in call report compliance. For banks with less than $500 million in assets, costs were similar regardless of the banks' size, but for banks with more than $500 million in assets, costs were significantly higher than for banks with less than $500 million in assets. Because the survey was of members and members are generally small, it did not contain evidence for call report compliance costs for the largest banks, however. As noted above, regulators argue that the call reports are already tailored to reduce the burden on small banks.

Since S. 1484 leaves it to regulators to shorten the call report, and regulators are currently undergoing a statutorily required review to eliminate unnecessary items from the call report, it is unclear what additional effect S. 1484 would have beyond the current review. One could argue that it would signal to regulators that Congress desires the current review to result in a shorter call report.

CFPB Supervisory Threshold (S. 1484/S. 1910)[277]

Section 110 of S. 1484 (Section 911 of S. 1910) would increase the threshold at which insured depository institutions (including banks and savings associations) and insured credit unions would be subject to CFPB supervision from $10 billion in total assets to $50 billion in total assets. The legislation would also index the $50 billion level to the annual change in gross domestic product.

Bank and Credit Union Regulation

Banks, savings associations, and credit unions are regulated for *safety and soundness* as well as for *consumer compliance*. Safety and soundness, or *prudential*, regulation is intended to ensure an institution is managed to maintain profitability and avoid failure. The focus of consumer compliance regulation, by contrast, is ensuring institutions conform with applicable consumer protection and fair-lending laws. Prior to the Dodd-Frank Act, the federal banking regulators (the Federal Reserve Board, the Office of the Comptroller of the Currency, the Federal Deposit Insurance Corporation, and the National Credit Union Administration) were charged with the two-pronged mandate of regulating for both safety and soundness and consumer compliance. Pursuant to the Dodd-Frank Act, the CFPB acquired certain consumer compliance powers over banks and credit unions that vary based on whether the institution holds more or less than $10 billion in assets.

For institutions with *more than $10 billion* in assets, the CFPB is the primary regulator for consumer compliance, whereas safety and soundness regulation continues to be performed by the prudential regulator. As a regulator of larger entities, the CFPB has rulemaking, supervisory, and enforcement authorities. This means the CFPB can issue rules for a large bank to follow, examine the bank to ensure it is in compliance with these rules, and take enforcement actions (such as imposing fines) against banks that fail to comply. A large institution, therefore, has different regulators for consumer protection and safety and soundness.

For institutions with *$10 billion or less* in assets, the rulemaking, supervisory, and enforcement authorities for consumer protection are divided between the CFPB and a prudential regulator. The CFPB may issue rules that would apply to smaller institutions from authorities granted under the federal consumer financial protection laws. The prudential regulator, however, would maintain primary supervisory and enforcement authority for consumer protection. The CFPB has limited supervisory authority over smaller institutions; it can participate in examinations of smaller entities performed by the prudential regulator "on a sampling basis." The CFPB does not have enforcement powers over small entities, but it may refer potential enforcement actions against small entities to the entities' prudential regulators (the prudential regulators must respond to such a referral but are not bound to take any other substantive steps).

Policy Discussion

Approximately 120 banks and credit unions have over $10 billion in assets. If the threshold was increased to $50 billion, about 80 institutions that are currently subject to CFPB supervision would no longer be, with approximately 40 institutions remaining under CFPB supervision. Though small in number, the largest institutions hold the vast majority of the industry's total assets.

Supporters of the legislative proposals to raise the CFPB threshold argue that financial institutions are subject to overly burdensome examinations that require bank managers to invest time and other resources that, the supporters believe, could be better spent elsewhere. By raising the threshold, the institutions "would still be examined by their primary regulators who are required by law to enforce the CFPB rules and regulations" but, supporters contend, the institutions "wouldn't have to go through yet another exam with the CFPB in addition to the ones they already have to go through with their primary regulators."[278] A higher threshold could reduce the regulatory burden imposed on those banks but, in supporters' opinion, still ensure that the institutions would be examined for consumer compliance.

Critics of the proposal noted that exam cycles could be better coordinated to reduce the burden institutions faced, but did not support raising the CFPB threshold. They argue that some of the banks in the asset range that would no longer be primarily supervised by the CFPB were, in critics' opinions, "some of the worst violators of consumer protections" in the housing bubble, with IndyMac at approximately $30 billion in assets an example that they highlight.[279] Raising the threshold could lead to those entities being subject to less intensive consumer compliance supervision (though it would not affect the consumer protection rules with which an entity would be required to comply, just the supervision).

Operation Choke Point (H.R. 766, H.R. 2578, S.Con.Res. 11, and S. 1484/S. 1910)[280]

Operation Choke Point (OCP) was a Department of Justice (DOJ) initiative aimed at curbing Internet fraudsters operating in conjunction with third-party payment processors.[281] It is the subject of numerous bills. Section 126 of S. 1484 (Section 927 of S. 1910) would prohibit the Federal Deposit Insurance Corporation, the Office of the Comptroller of the Currency, the Board of Governors of the Federal Reserve, the Bureau of Consumer Financial Protection, and the National Credit Union Administration from implementing or participating in Operation Choke Point.

The Financial Institution Consumer Protection Act of 2015 (H.R. 766) passed the House on February 4, 2016. It would bar banking regulators from formally requesting or informally suggesting that a depository bank close customer accounts unless the regulators have a *material reason*[282] for the request, which cannot be based solely on reputational risk. The bill also identifies several threats that could satisfy the material reason requirement; specifically, if the customer

- poses a threat to national security;
- is engaged in terrorism financing;
- is doing business with Iran, North Korea, Syria, or another State Sponsor of Terrorism;[283]
- or is doing business with an entity in any of those countries.

The bill would require depository institutions to inform their customers of the justification for account termination. The bill would also require the regulators to report annually to Congress the number of accounts terminated at the request of the regulator and the legal justification for the request.

Other legislative proposals also address OCP. The Commerce, Justice, Science, and Related Agencies Appropriations Act, 2016 (H.R. 2578), which passed the House on June 3, 2015, would prohibit funds provided by H.R. 2578 from being used for OCP. The budget resolution for FY2016 (S.Con.Res. 11) includes a provision for a non-binding deficit-neutral reserve fund to end OCP.[284]

Operation Choke Point

According to DOJ, OCP's stated goal was "to attack Internet, telemarketing, mail, and other mass market fraud against consumers, by choking fraudsters' access to the banking system." [285] While OCP remained a DOJ initiative, DOJ did communicate with other law enforcement agencies and financial regulators to ensure it had all the information needed to evaluate the enforcement options available to address the violations.[286] The operation held banks and payments processors accountable for processing transactions that they knew were fraudulent.[287] Fraud may be committed by scammers who take advantage of increased online commerce to systemically extract money from consumers' bank accounts. According to DOJ, once a fraudulent merchant enters the banking system, they can debit consumers bank accounts and credit their own account repeatedly, without permission and in violation of federal law, unless someone stops them.[288] The DOJ has sought legal action in certain circumstances that has resulted in civil monetary penalty fees levied against financial institutions who, despite indications of fraud, continued to process fraudulent merchant transactions-in violation of federal law.[289]

Policy Discussion

One of the major issues related to OCP is whether it affected businesses that are lawful and legitimate. Allegedly, DOJ and bank regulators labeled certain firms as high-risk, including credit repair companies, debt consolidation and forgiveness programs, online gambling-related operations, government-grant or will-writing kits, pornography, online tobacco or firearm sales, pharmaceutical sales, sweepstakes, magazine subscriptions, and payday or subprime loans. Certain bank regulators also considered some of these merchants to pose a *reputational risk*[290] to the financial institutions that provide services to these merchants.[291] Federal banking regulators have also supported DOJ efforts either through guidance or policy statements. As an example, Federal Deposit Insurance Cooperation's *Guidance on Payment Processor Relationships* recommended banks to conduct heightened scrutiny of certain types of accounts.[292]

Some have argued that, contrary to DOJ public statements, OCP was primarily focused on the payday lending industry.[293] In addition, they contend that DOJ was pressuring banks to shut down accounts without proving the merchants using the banking services broke the laws. They further assert, in instances when the banks did not shut down the accounts, DOJ has penalized the banks for wrongdoing that may or may not have happened.[294]

Based on the staff report by the Committee on Oversight and Government Reform and a letter from Members of Congress,[295] DOJ's Office of Professional Responsibility performed a review of OCP. The review concluded that

> Department of Justice attorneys did not improperly target lawful participants involved in the Internet payday lending industry ... To the extent that Civil Division attorneys involved in Operation Choke Point investigated Internet payday lending, their focus appeared to be on only a small number of lenders they had reason to suspect were engaged in fraudulent practices.[296]

The review found some evidence indicating that "some of the congressional and industry concerns relating to Internet payday lending was understandable," including some DOJ memoranda disparaging payday lending and emails indicating that "some of the attorneys ... working on Operation Choke Point may have viewed Internet payday lending in a negative light."[297] The review "did not find evidence of an effort to improperly pressure lawful businesses," although it did find that "attorneys at one point did enclose with ... subpoenas ... regulatory guidance from federal regulators, including one document that contained a footnote listing businesses that the FDIC had described as posing an 'elevated risk.' [298] The review concluded OCP did not compel banks to terminate their relationship with legitimate businesses.[299]

In addition, an audit by the FDIC's Inspector General found that the "FDIC's involvement in Operation Choke Point to have been inconsequential to the overall direction and outcome of the initiative."[300]

To address concerns raised by Congress and the financial services industry about OCP, FDIC issued new guidance and removed the list of examples of merchants categories that were considered high risk. Further, FDIC has established dedicated email, and a toll-free number for the Office of the Ombudsman for institutions to address any concerns raised by FDIC supervised institutions about OCP.[301]

CBO's cost estimates for H.R. 766 as ordered to be reported determined that the legislative proposals would have no effect on the federal budget.[302]

CAPITAL ISSUANCE

Banks face regulations surrounding how they can raise capital from investors, and what rights are conferred to investors. Capital can take various forms depending on the ownership structure of the institution. For example, publicly-held banks issue stock that can be traded on exchanges. Disclosure requirements and investor protections may better inform investors about the risks that they are assuming, but can make it more costly for institutions to raise capital, and those costs might be passed on to customers in the form of higher fees or interest rates charged. While some view these existing regulatory requirements as important safeguards that ensure that investors are protected from fraud, others see them as unnecessary red tape that makes it too difficult for banks to raise the capital needed to expand or remain healthy.

Holding Company Registration Threshold Equalization (H.R. 22, H.R. 37, H.R. 1334, and S. 1484/S. 1910)[303]

Four bills that have seen congressional action would raise the exemption threshold on the Securities and Exchange Commission's (SEC's) registration for thrift holding companies to match the current exemptions for bank holding companies (BHCs). The proposal is found in the Holding Company Registration Threshold Equalization Act (H.R. 1334), which passed the House on July 15, 2015; Title III of the Promoting Job Creation and Reducing Small Business Burdens Act (H.R. 37), which passed the House on January 14, 2015; the Fixing America's Surface Transportation Act (H.R. 22/P.L. 114-94); and Section 601 of S. 1484 (which is also Section 971 of S. 1910).

Background

Historically, under the Securities Act of 1933,[304] banks and BHCs, similar to nonfinancial firms, generally were required to register securities with the SEC if they had total assets exceeding $10 million and the shares were held (as per shareholders of record) by 500 shareholders or more. Banks and BHCs also were allowed to stop registering securities with the SEC, a process known as *deregistration*, if the number of their shareholders of record fell to 300 shareholders or fewer.

Title VI of the Jumpstart Our Business Startups Act (JOBS Act)[305] raised the SEC shareholder registration threshold from 500 shareholders to 2,000 shareholders and increased the upper limit for deregistration from 300 shareholders to 1,200 shareholders for those banks and nonfinancial firms. In other words, the JOBS Act made it easier for banks and BHCs to increase the number of their shareholders while remaining unregistered private banks and, if already registered, to voluntarily deregister while also adding more shareholders.[306] The provision went into effect immediately upon the enactment of the JOBS Act on April 5, 2012.

These changes made by the JOBS Act did not apply to savings and loan holding companies (SLHCs). H.R. 37/S. 1484 /S. 1910 would amend the Securities Exchange Act of 1934[307] by extending the higher registration and deregistration shareholder thresholds in the JOBS Act for banks and BHCs to SLHCs. Savings and loans (also known as thrifts and savings banks) are similar to banks in that they take deposits and make loans, but their regulation is somewhat different. Over time, the differences between banks and savings and loans have narrowed.[308] Under the provision, an SLHC would be required to register with the SEC if its assets exceed $10 million and it has 2,000 shareholders of record, up from the current requirement of 500 shareholders of record. SLHCs that want to deregister from the SEC would have to have no more than 1,200 shareholders of record, an increase over the current 300 or fewer shareholders.

Policy Discussion

Generally speaking, the central perceived benefit of SEC registration is to enhance investor protection by ensuring that investors have access to significant financial and nonfinancial data about firms and the securities they issue. The cost of SEC registration is the regulatory burden on the firm issuing securities associated with complying with SEC requirements, which potentially raises the cost of capital and reduces how much capital a firm can raise. For small firms, the regulatory burden of registration is thought to be greater than for larger firms.[309]

Policymakers attempt to reach the optimal trade-off between costs and benefits of SEC registration by exempting firms below a certain size from registration requirements. The JOBS Act raised this threshold for banks, modifying the balance between costs and benefits.

Reports indicate that after passage of the JOBS Act, a number of privately held banks and BHCs took advantage of Title VI's reduction in shareholder ownership registration triggers by raising capital from additional shareholders without having to register with the SEC.[310] Some banks also have taken the opportunity to deregister from the SEC.[311] One of the few studies on changes to the financial health of banks that took advantage of the JOBS Act threshold changes to deregister found that the act was generally, but not entirely, financially beneficial to banks. For example, it found that, on average, the legislation resulted in $1.31 in higher net bank income and $3.28 lower pretax expenses for every $1.00 of bank assets and was responsible for $1.54 million in increased assets per bank employee.[312] The study did not attempt to estimate the costs to investors of reduced disclosure under the changes made by the JOBS Act.

In potentially expanding the exemption threshold on SEC registration for thrift holding companies, there are two main points to consider. First, should exemption levels from SEC registration requirements be different for thrifts and savings and loans than for banks? Current law makes it more difficult for small thrifts to raise capital than for small banks. Second, are the costs and benefits of registration requirements for small banks better balanced at the higher thresholds enacted for banks in the JOBS Act or the lower thresholds in current law for thrifts?

Mutual Holding Company Dividend Waivers (S. 1484/S. 1910)[313]

Section 113 of S. 1484 (Section 914 of S. 1910) addresses the issue of how dividends are allocated among the shareholders of mutual holding companies or their subsidiaries.

Mutual Holding Companies (MHCs)

Section 107 of the Competitive Equality Banking Act of 1987[314] provided for the formation of Mutual Holding Companies (MHCs). MHCs are savings and loan holding companies in mutual form, some of which own mutually held federally insured savings and loan associations, and state-chartered mutual savings banks. Most banks in the United States are held either publicly or privately by shareholders. In contrast, a mutual company or mutual savings bank (association) is one that is owned by its members. In the instance of a mutual savings bank, the members are the financial institution's depositors.[315] A mutual savings bank can reorganize itself into an MHC by transferring all of the assets and liabilities to a newly formed stock institution, the majority shares of which are owned by the MHC. The remaining minority shares are sold to equity investors, with depositors afforded the right to buy minority equity interest before it is made available to the public.[316]

The Dodd-Frank Act transferred authority over savings and loan holding companies regulated by the Office of Thrift Supervision (OTS) to the Federal

Reserve[317] and included a specific provision which requires a MHC to follow certain procedures in order to waive receipt of any dividend declared by a subsidiary.[318] Dividends are distribution of earnings (profits) to shareholders, which are usually declared and paid quarterly. The board of directors determines the amount of dividends. If the MHC waives the right to receive dividends, depending upon the specifics of an institution's dividend arrangements, dividends may be distributed among the other equity holders or retained by the bank subsidiary.

The Federal Reserve issued Regulation MM, implementing its authority over MHCs[319] and included in it a subsection, 12 C.F.R. 239.8(d), implementing the statutory requirements permitting MHCs to waive the right to receive dividends declared by a subsidiary of the MHC. Under the Federal Reserve regulations,

> an MHC may waive the right to receive any dividend declared by a subsidiary... if (i) no insider of the MHC, associate of an insider, or tax-qualified or non-tax-qualified employee stock benefit plan of the MHC holds any share of the stock in the class of stock to which the waiver would apply, or (ii) the MHC gives written notice to the ... [Federal Reserve] of the intent of the MHC to waive the right to receive dividends ... and the [Federal Reserve] Board does not object.[320]

The regulation specifies what must be included in the notice of waiver, including documentation of the MHC's conclusion that a waiver would be consistent with the fiduciary duties of the board of directors of the MHC.

The Dodd-Frank Act and the Federal Reserve regulation include a streamlined approval process for dividend waivers by certain "grandfathered MHC's." Under the statute, the Federal Reserve may not object to a proposed waiver of dividends for an MHC that waived dividends prior to December 1, 2009, (grandfathered MHC's) provided "the waiver would not be detrimental to the safe and sound operation of the ... [mutual savings bank]"; and, the MHC's board "expressly determines the waiver to be consistent with its fiduciary duties to the mutual members of the MHC."[321] For MHCs that do not meet the criteria for grandfathering, Regulation MM specifies conditions under which the Federal Reserve will not object to a waiver of dividends for non-grandfathered MHCs. Among them are a vote of the members of the MHC approving the waiver of dividends; a determination that the mutual savings bank is operating in a safe and sound manner, which will not be jeopardized by the waiver; and an affirmation that the MHC is able to meet any obligations in connection with any loan for which the MHC has pledged the stock of the subsidiary mutual savings bank.[322]

Section 113 of S. 1484 (Section 914 of S. 1910) authorizes all MHCs to waive the "receipt of dividends declared on the common stock of their bank or mid-size holding company" without having to comply the Federal Reserve's regulation regarding "Mutual Holding Company Dividend Waivers."[323]

Policy Discussion

In prior circumstances, the Federal Reserve identified a number of issues related to dividend waivers by the holding company. One of the reasons for retaining dividends is so the MHC could serve as a source of strength to its subsidiary bank. If the MHC retains the dividend payments from the subsidiary, then an MHC can transfer its excess capital to the subsidiary when the subsidiary might need a capital infusion.[324] If there is no requirement for a mandatory vote of MHC shareholders, the waiver would rest exclusively with the board or of the MHC, who may have a financial interest in the waiver as minority shareholders in the bank.

In issuing the regulations implementing the Dodd-Frank dividend waiver provisions, the Federal Reserve also noted that dividend waiver by the MHC without corresponding waiver by the minority (i.e., non-member) shareholders poses an "inherent conflict of interest" because it might result in unequal distribution of equity between mutual owners of the MHC and minority shareholders. In essence, it could result in a transfer of equity from mutual owners to minority shareholders.[325]

Supporters of S. 1484 cite similar reasons as those that opposed the implementation of Regulation MM's dividend waiver requirements in 2011.[326] They fear that the Fed will erroneously block waivers under Regulation MM, thereby harming MHCs and discouraging capital formation. They assert that if the MHC waives the dividends, greater capital is retained by the subsidiary, which would enhance the safe and sound operation of the subsidiary savings bank. Further, they state, waiving dividends for majority shareholders while retaining them for minority shareholders may be necessary in order to offer the latter a market rate of return. Lastly, the supporters state that when the MHC receives the dividends from the subsidiary it must pay taxes on the dividends received, thereby reducing the overall franchise value.[327]

The supporters of S. 1484 also state that by distinguishing between grandfathered MHCs and the rest of the MHCs lead to different classes of MHCs. They also assert that the cost of obtaining the vote of the members could be cost prohibitive and lead to additional unnecessary administrative and financial costs.[328]

Previously, in similar circumstances, the banking regulators have allowed waiver of dividends by the MHC and those dividends to be retained by the bank. In such instances, the regulators required specific accounting procedures to allocate the value of those dividends to the members of the mutual institution. This process helped delineate the increase in value of the MHC to be properly apportioned between the members and minority shareholders.[329]

APPENDIX A. INDEXING OF BANK REGULATORY RELIEF PROVISIONS FOR GDP GROWTH

Certain provisions of S. 1484/S. 1910 with exemptions based on size are indexed by "such amount is adjusted annually...to reflect the percentage change for the previous calendar year in the gross domestic product of the United States, as calculated by the Bureau of Economic Analysis of the Department of Commerce." Indexing reduces the number of firms that "graduate" from the exemption over time as they grow in size, in nominal or real terms. Nominal price increases are caused by inflation, whereas real price increases refer to those in excess of the inflation rate. Table A-1 summarizes those provisions that apply to banks.

Table A-1. Provisions Indexed for GDP Growth

Section of S. 1484	Section of S. 1910	Topic	Current and Proposed Threshold (billions)
110(a)	911(a)	Exemption from swap clearing requirements for banks, savings associations, farm credit system institutions, and credit unions below the threshold	$10
110(b)	911(b)	Depository institutions and credit unions above the threshold subject to CFPB supervision	$10 to $50
110(c)	911(c)	Exemption from security-based swap clearing requirements for banks, savings associations, farm credit system institutions, and credit unions below the threshold	$10

Section of S. 1484	Section of S. 1910	Topic	Current and Proposed Threshold (billions)
110(d)	911(d)	Exemption from debit interchange fee restrictions for issuers below the threshold("Durbin Amendment")	$10
110(e)	911(e)	Offset of increased deposit insurance assessments for banks below the threshold	$10
110(f)	911(f)	Exemption from executive compensation standards for depository institutions, broker-dealers, credit unions, investment advisors, Fannie Mae, Freddie Mac, and other financial institutions designated by regulators below the threshold	$1
115	916	Exemption from Volcker Rule for banks below the threshold	$10
201	931	Exemption from enhanced prudential regulation for bank holding companies below $50billion, eligible for designation if between $50billionand $500billion, automatically subject to enhanced prudential regulation if above $500billion	$50, $500
202	932	Risk committee requirements apply to publicly-traded bank holding companies above the threshold	$10 to $50
202	932	Company-run stress test requirements apply to banks above the threshold	$10 to $50
n/a	928	Grants regulators discretion to exempt banks below the threshold from certain regulations	$10

Source: CRS analysis.

Note: Threshold is based on total assets, unless otherwise noted.

Section 110 of S. 1484 (Section 911 of S. 1910) indexes exemptions found in a few provisions of existing law (all added by the Dodd-Frank Act) while making no other changes to those provisions, except 110(b), which also raised the threshold and is discussed in the section above entitled "CFPB Supervisory Threshold." The other exemptions are found within other sections of the bills that make broader changes to current law. In addition, Section 108 of S. 1484 (Section 909 of S. 1910) indexed thresholds for exemptions from points and fees for manufactured housing for inflation (as measured by the consumer price index) instead of GDP.

GDP is revised repeatedly and is not available on the first of the year, so regulators would have to formulate a method for making this calculation. The bills do not specify whether regulators should use the nominal or real GDP growth rate—nominal GDP growth is equal to real GDP growth plus the inflation rate. If regulators used the real GDP growth rate, GDP in some years could be negative or lower than the inflation rate. In most years, GDP grows faster than inflation, so the thresholds would be increasing in real terms over the long run. Total assets of the financial system also generally increase more rapidly than inflation, so indexing by GDP growth instead of inflation would make it less likely that an increasing number of firms would not be subject to the exemption over time.

APPENDIX B. PROVISIONS IN THE FINANCIAL REGULATORY IMPROVEMENT ACT COVERED IN THIS REPORT

Table B-1 lists the provisions in S. 1484, the Financial Regulatory Improvement Act, that are covered in this report and the corresponding section in S. 1910, Financial Services and General Government Appropriations Act, 2016, and related House bills.

Table B-1. Provisions in the Financial Regulatory Improvement Act Covered in this Report

Subject	S. 1484	S. 1910	Related House Bill
Privacy Notifications	Section 101	Section 902	H.R. 601, H.R. 22
Rural Lending	Section 103	Section 904	H.R. 1259, H.R. 22
Exam Ombudsman and Appeals Process	Section 104	Section 905	H.R. 1941
Portfolio Qualified Mortgage	Section 106	Section 907	H.R. 1210
Points and Fees	Section 107	Section 908	H.R. 685
Manufactured Housing	Section 108	Section 909	H.R. 650
Exam Frequency for Small Banks	Section 109	Section 910	H.R. 1553, H.R. 22
CFPB Supervisory Threshold	Section 110	Section 911	n/a
Mutual Holding Company Dividend Waivers	Section 113	Section 914	n/a
Volcker Rule, Exemption for Community Banks	Section 115	Section 916	n/a

Subject	S. 1484	S. 1910	Related House Bill
Capital Treatment of Mortgage Servicing Assets	Section 116	Section 917	H.R. 1408
Integrated Disclosure Forms	Section 117	Section 918	H.R. 3192
Call Report Reform	Section 119	Section 920	
Change to the "Collins Amendment"	Section 123	Section 924	H.R. 22
EGRPRA Process	Section 125	Section 926	n/a
Operation Choke Point	Section 126	Section 927	H.R. 766, H.R. 2578
Thresholds for Enhanced Regulation	Section 201	Section 931	H.R. 1309
Holding Company Registration Threshold Equalization	Section 601	Section 971	H.R. 37, H.R. 22, H.R. 1334

Source: Table created by CRS.

Notes: S. 1910, Section 928 ("Exemptive Authority") is the only provision of S. 1910 discussed in this report that was not originally part of S. 1484. "Related House Bill" only includes bills covered in this report.

Appendix C. Provisions in the Fixing America's Surface Transportation Act Covered in this Report

H.R. 22, the Fixing America's Surface Transportation Act, was signed into law as P.L. 114-94 on December 4, 2015. Division G of H.R. 22 contained 19 titles related to financial services. Table C-1 lists the provisions of Division G that are covered in this report and the corresponding section in S. 1484 and related House bills.

Table C-1. Provisions in the Fixing America's Surface Transportation Act Covered in this Report

Subject	Title of H.R. 22	Section of S. 1484	Related House Bill
Privacy Notifications	LXXV	101	H.R. 601
Exam Frequency for Small Banks	LXXXIII	109	H.R. 1553
Holding Company Registration	LXXXV	601	H.R. 37, H.R. 3791
Threshold Equalization			
Change to the "Collins Amendment"	LXXXVII	123	n/a
Rural Lending	LXXXIX	103	H.R. 1259

Source: Table created by CRS.

End Notes

[1] For a summary of the regulatory relief debate, see CRS In Focus IF10162, *Introduction to Financial Services: "Regulatory Relief"*, by Sean M. Hoskins and Marc Labonte.

[2] P.L. 111-203.

[3] For a summary, see CRS Report R41350, *The Dodd-Frank Wall Street Reform and Consumer Protection Act: Background and Summary*, coordinated by Baird Webel.

[4] Congressional Budget Office, *Cost Estimate of* S. 1484, July 29, 2015, at https://www.cbo.gov/sites/default/files/ 114th-congress-2015-2016/costestimate/s1484.pdf.

[5] These provisions are discussed below in the section entitled "Thresholds for Enhanced Regulation S. 1484/S. 1910."

[6] Some of the bills addressed in this report would modify a regulation that applies to banks and nonbanks engaged in a specific activity.

[7] For an analysis of the regulatory burden on small banks, see CRS Report R43999, *An Analysis of the Regulatory Burden on Small Banks*, by Sean M. Hoskins and Marc Labonte.

[8] This section was authored by Marc Labonte, specialist in Macroeconomic Policy, and Edward V. Murphy, specialist in Financial Economics.

[9] P.L. 111-203, §619. For more information, see CRS Legal Sidebar, *What Companies Must Comply with the Volcker Rule?*, David H. Carpenter.

[10] For a summary of the Volcker Rule, see Federal Reserve, "Final Rules to Implement the 'Volcker Rule,'" at http://www.federalreserve.gov/newsevents/press/bcreg/bcreg20131210 a3.pdf.

[11] "Prohibitions and Restrictions on Proprietary Trading and Certain Interests," 79 *Federal Register* 5778, January 31, 2014.

[12] Federal Deposit Insurance Corporation (FDIC), *The Volcker Rule: Community Bank App*, at https://www.fdic.gov/ regulations/reform/volcker/summary.html.

[13] Gov. Daniel Tarullo, "A Tiered Approach to Regulation and Supervision of Community Banks," speech at the Community Bankers Symposium, Chicago, Illinois, November, 7, 2014, at http://www.federalreserve.gov/newsevents/ speech/tarullo20141107a.htm.

[14] Thomas Hoenig, speech at the National Press Club, April 15, 2015, at https://www.fdic.gov/ news/news/speeches/spapril1515.html.

[15] U.S. Congress, House Committee on Financial Services, Subcommittee on Capital Markets and Government Sponsored Enterprises, *The Dodd-Frank Act's Impact on Asset-Backed Securities*, Testimony of Meredith Coffey, 113th Cong., 2nd sess., February 26, 2014.

[16] See CRS Legal Sidebar, *Congress Contemplates Extending Volcker Rule Conformance Period for CLO Investments*, David H. Carpenter.

[17] See CRS Legal Sidebar, *What Companies Must Comply with the Volcker Rule?*, David H. Carpenter.

[18] Hamilton Place Strategies, *Regulating Risk: Implementation of New Regulation*, January 2015, at http://hamiltonplacestrategies.com/sites/default/files/newsfiles/HPS%20White%20 Paper%20- %20Regulating%20Risk%20-%20Volcker%20and%20CLOs.pdf.

[19] Executive Office of the President, *Statement of Administrative Policy*, January 12, 2015, at http://www.whitehouse.gov/sites/default/files/omb/legislative/sap/114/saphr37r_20150112. pdf.

[20] This section was authored by Marc Labonte, specialist in Macroeconomic Policy.

[21] The regulation implementing this section places limits on the share of grandfathered instruments that can be used to meet capital requirements. See Office of the Comptroller of the Currency and Federal Reserve System, "Regulatory Capital Rules," 78 *Federal*

Register, October 11, 2013, p. 62052, http://www.gpo.gov/fdsys/pkg/FR-2013-10-11/pdf/2013-21653.pdf.

[22] Richard Wald, Emigrant Bank, Testimony Before U.S. Congress, House Committee on Financial Services, Subcommittee on Financial Institutions and Consumer Credit, *The Impact of the Dodd-Frank Act*, 112th Cong., 2nd sess., May 18, 2012.http://financial services.house.gov/calendar/eventsingle.aspx?EventID=295210. This provision was included in H.R. 3128 in the 112th Congress.

[23] This section was authored by Marc Labonte, specialist in Macroeconomic Policy.

[24] This section is similar to S. 1799. It is the only provision of S. 1910 discussed in this report that was not originally part of S. 1484.

[25] In a recent speech, Fed Gov. Tarullo gave some examples of policies where he thought a size exemption might be warranted but the law did not permit it. Gov. Daniel Tarullo, "A Tiered Approach to Regulation and Supervision of Community Banks," speech at the Community Bankers Symposium, Chicago, Illinois, November, 7, 2014, at http://www.federalreserve.gov/newsevents/speech/tarullo20141107a.htm.

[26] This section was authored by Sean Hoskins, analyst in Financial Economics.

[27] H.R. 1408, §2.

[28] H.R. 1408, §2.

[29] For more on Basel, see CRS Report R42744, *U.S. Implementation of the Basel Capital Regulatory Framework*, by Darryl E. Getter. The National Credit Union Administration (NCUA) has a similar capital rule for credit unions. See NCUA, "Risk-Based Capital," 80 *Federal Register* 17, January 27, 2015.

[30] Although banks have begun implementing the Basel III capital rules already, including the new mortgage servicing asset (MSA) treatment, the new treatment will not be fully phased in for several years. See Federal Reserve, Office of the Comptroller of the Currency, "Regulatory Capital Rules," 78 *Federal Register* 62079, October 11, 2013.

[31] For more on the market shift to nonbank servicers, see Laurie Goodman and Pamela Lee, *OASIS: A Securitization Born from MSR Transfers*, Urban Institute, at http://www.urban.org/sites/default/files/alfresco/publication-pdfs/413086-OASIS-A-Securitization-Born-from-MSR-Transfers.PDF.

[32] For more information, see CRS Report R42572, *The Consumer Financial Protection Bureau (CFPB): A Legal Analysis*, by David H. Carpenter.

[33] Benjamin Lawsky, "Excerpts from Superintendent Lawsky's Remarks on Non-Bank Mortgage Servicing in New York City," May 20, 2014, at http://www.dfs.ny.gov/about/press2014/pr1405201.htm.

[34] Attributed to Rep. Ed Perlmutter by CQ Congressional Transcripts, "House Financial Services Committee Holds Markup on Financial Regulatory Legislation," March 25, 2015, at http://www.cq.com/doc/financialtranscripts4653577?9&search=M9QutUd4.

[35] See American Bankers Association, "Letter to Representatives Luetkemeyer and Perlmutter," May 12, 2014, at http://www.aba.com/Advocacy/LetterstoCongress/Documents/ABA LetteronMSAStop-StudyBill.pdf.

[36] Attributed to Rep. Maxine Waters by CQ Congressional Transcripts, "House Financial Services Committee Holds Markup on Financial Regulatory Legislation," March 25, 2015, at http://www.cq.com/doc/financialtranscripts4653577?9&search=M9QutUd4.

[37] CQ Congressional Transcripts, "House Financial Services Committee Holds Markup on Financial Regulatory Legislation, March 25, 2015, at http://www.cq.com/doc/financial transcripts-4653577?9&search=M9QutUd4.

[38] CBO, *Cost Estimate of* H.R. 1408, April 9, 2015, at https://www.cbo.gov/sites/default/ files/cbofiles/attachments/ hr1408_1.pdf.

[39] This section was authored by Marc Labonte, specialist in Macroeconomic Policy.

[40] FSOC is a council of financial regulators, headed by the Treasury Secretary, that was created by the Dodd-Frank Act.

[41] A current list of top 50 holding companies by asset size is available at http://www.ffiec.gov/nicpubweb/nicweb/ Top50Form.aspx. Some of the firms on this list are not bank holding companies. Savings and loan (thrift) holding companies with more than $50 billion in assets are not subject to the final rule, but the Fed has indicated that it intends to propose rulemaking in the future that apply to them.

[42] To date, the Fed and FSOC have not chosen to increase the threshold from $50 billion.

[43] FSOC issued a rule in 2015 increasing the transparency of the non-bank designation process and permitting the company under consideration greater opportunities for input. For more information, see CRS Legal Sidebar WSLG1190, *FSOC Announces Rule Change to Increase Transparency in Designating SIFIs*, by M. Maureen Murphy.

[44] Using G-SIB designation as the criteria for automatic U.S. designation could potentially lead to the designation of some foreign headquartered G-SIBs that are not currently subject to some of Dodd-Frank's enhanced regulations because they have less than $50 billion in assets in U.S. banking entities. The Fed would then need to decide whether to apply some or all of the existing enhanced prudential regulations to the newly designated G-SIBs.

[45] Financial Stability Board, http://www.fsb.org/wp-content/uploads/2015-update-of-list-of-global-systemicallyimportant-banks-G-SIBs.pdf. The Financial Stability Board is an inter-governmental organization that monitors and develops standards for the global financial system.

[46] The rule, "Enhanced Prudential Standards for Bank Holding Companies and Foreign Banking Organizations," can be accessed at http://federalreserve.gov/newsevents/press/ bcreg/20140218a.htm.

[47] For more information, see CRS Report R42150, *Systemically Important or "Too Big to Fail" Financial Institutions*, by Marc Labonte.

[48] For a detailed discussion of tiered regulation for large banks, see Daniel Tarullo, testimony before the Senate Banking Committee, March 19, 2015, at http://www.banking.senate.gov/ public/index.cfm?FuseAction=Files.View& FileStore_id=2f189eda-33df-41e4-a2cd-a41c63d34499.

[49] The Congressional Research Service was not able to locate an official list of banks subject to Title I enhanced supervision. In 2015, 31 BHCs were subject to the Title I Federal Reserve stress tests because they had over $50 billion in assets. See Federal Reserve, *Dodd-Frank Act Stress Test 2015*, March 2015, http://www.federalreserve.gov/ newsevents/press/bcreg/ bcreg20150305a1.pdf. About 130 banks (foreign and domestic) have submitted resolution plans ("living wills") pursuant to Title I, however. See Chairman Martin Gruenberg, testimony before the Senate Committee on Banking, Housing, and Urban Affairs, September 9, 2014, p. 5, available at http://www.banking.senate.gov/public/ index.cfm?FuseAction=Hearings.Testimony&Hearing_ID=b15fc832-df18- 47d7-8c7d-1367e5770086&Witness_ID=c15856a4-8f8c-4958-ad7c-a385bb31c3f8.

[50] See, for example, Deron Smithy, testimony before the Senate Banking Committee, March 24, 2015, at http://www.banking.senate.gov/public/index.cfm?FuseAction=Files.View&FileStore_id=14d286e0-9c50-4b96-87cffe999112550f. The argument that regional banks have a traditional business model has been disputed. See, for example, Simon Johnson, testimony before the Senate Banking Committee, March 24, 2015, at http://www.banking.senate.gov/

public/index.cfm?FuseAction=Files.View&FileStore_id=14d286e0-9c50-4b96-87cf-fe999112550f.

[51] Simon Johnson, testimony before the Senate Banking Committee, March 24, 2015, at http://www.banking.senate.gov/public/index.cfm?FuseAction=Files.View&FileStore_id=14d286e0-9c50-4b96-87cffe999112550f.

[52] This section was authored by Sean Hoskins, analyst in Financial Economics.

[53] P.L. 104-208, 12 U.S.C. §3311.

[54] OCC, Federal Reserve, FDIC, "Regulatory Publication and Review Under the Economic Growth and Regulatory Paperwork Reduction Act of 1996," 80 *Federal Register* 7980, February 13, 2015.

[55] OCC, Federal Reserve, FDIC, "Regulatory Publication and Review Under the Economic Growth and Regulatory Paperwork Reduction Act of 1996," 79 *Federal Register* 32173, June 4, 2014. Regulations under review can be found at FFIEC, "Regulations Under Review," at http://egrpra.ffiec.gov/regulations-under-review/regulations-under-review-index.html. The previous report can be accessed at FFIEC, *Joint Report to Congress: EGRPRA*, July 31, 2007, p. 30, at http://egrpra.ffiec.gov/docs/egrpra-joint-report.pdf.

[56] NCUA, "Regulatory Publication and Review Under the Economic Growth and Regulatory Paperwork Reduction Act of 1996," 79 *Federal Register* 75763, December 19, 2014.

[57] OCC, Federal Reserve, FDIC, "Regulatory Publication and Review Under the Economic Growth and Regulatory Paperwork Reduction Act of 1996," 80 *Federal Register* 7980, February 13, 2015.

[58] OCC, Federal Reserve, FDIC, "Regulatory Publication and Review Under the Economic Growth and Regulatory Paperwork Reduction Act of 1996," 79 *Federal Register* 32174, June 4, 2014.

[59] Ibid.

[60] Federal Reserve, FDIC, OCC, "Agencies Announce Additional EGRPRA Outreach Meetings," press release, April 6, 2015, at http://www.federalreserve.gov/newsevents/press/bcreg/20150406a.htm.

[61] Better Markets, *Regulatory Publication and Review under the Economic Growth and Regulatory Paperwork Reduction Act of 1996 ("EGRPRA")*, March 14, 2015, at http://www.federalreserve.gov/SECRS/2015/May/20150522/R-1510/R-1510%20_051415_129942_418572489457_1.pdf.

[62] Ibid.

[63] Sen. Mike Crapo, "Crapo: Dodd-Frank, CFPB Rules Must Be Included in 10-Year Regulatory Review," press release, March 27, 2015, at http://www.crapo.senate.gov/media/newsreleases/release_full.cfm?id=358726.

[64] This section was authored by Marc Labonte, specialist in Macroeconomic Policy.

[65] For more information, see CRS Report R44146, *The Demand for Municipal Bonds: Issues for Congress*, by Darryl E. Getter and Raj Gnanarajah.

[66] Congressional Budget Office, *Cost Estimate,* January 15, 2016, at https://www.cbo.gov/sites/default/files/114thcongress-2015-2016/costestimate/hr2209.pdf.

[67] Office of the Comptroller of the Currency, Federal Reserve System, Federal Deposit Insurance Corporation, "Liquidity Coverage Ratio," 79 *Federal Register* 197, October 10, 2014, at https://www.gpo.gov/fdsys/pkg/FR-2014 10-10/pdf/2014-22520.pdf. For more information, see CRS In Focus IF10208, *The Liquidity Coverage Ratio (LCR)*, by Marc Labonte.

[68] Outflows are measured net of inflows because market stress might cause funds to flow into a bank as well as flow out.

[69] The final rule differs from the Basel III agreement, which allowed some municipal bonds to count as Level 2A HQLA. Office of the Comptroller of the Currency (OCC), Federal Reserve System, Federal Deposit Insurance Corporation (FDIC), "Liquidity Coverage Ratio," 79 *Federal Register* 197, October 10, 2014, p. 61463, at https://www.gpo.gov/fdsys/pkg/FR-2014-10-10/pdf/2014-22520.pdf.

[70] Federal Reserve, press release, May 21, 2015, at http://www.federalreserve.gov/newsevents/press/bcreg/ 20150521a.htm.

[71] Dedicated revenue bonds are bonds issued by public entities that are repaid through a pre-identified stream of future revenues. Insured bonds are municipal bonds whose principal and interest has been insured by private firms. Insured bonds were not included as HQLA because several bond insurers failed during the financial crisis.

[72] Demand could be further reduced if the rule is extended to non-bank SIFIs in the future.

[73] Federal Reserve, *Financial Accounts of the United States*, December 10, 2015, Table L. 212, at http://www.federalreserve.gov/releases/z1/current/z1.pdf.

[74] Municipal Securities Rulemaking Board, *2014 Fact Book*, 2015, pp. 23-24, at http://www.msrb.org/msrb1/pdfs/ MSRB-Fact-Book-2014.pdf.

[75] Office of the Comptroller of the Currency (OCC), Federal Reserve System, Federal Deposit Insurance Corporation (FDIC), "Liquidity Coverage Ratio," 79 *Federal Register* 197, October 10, 2014, p. 61462, at https://www.gpo.gov/ fdsys/pkg/FR-2014-10-10/pdf/2014-22520.pdf.

[76] OCC, Federal Reserve System, FDIC, "Liquidity Coverage Ratio," 79 *Federal Register* 197, October 10, 2014, p. 61463, at https://www.gpo.gov/fdsys/pkg/FR-2014-10-10/pdf/2014-22520.pdf.

[77] Securities Industry and Financial Markets Association, *Comment Letter*, July 24, 2015, at http://www.cecouncil.com/media/245151/sifma-submits-comments-to-the-federal-reserve-system-on-the-liquidity-coverage-ratio-rule.pdf.

[78] This section was authored by Marc Labonte, specialist in Macroeconomic Policy.

[79] Appendix C to 12 C.F.R. §225.

[80] These requirements are discussed at Federal Reserve, "Small Bank Holding Company Policy Statement," 80 *Federal Register* 20156, April 15, 2015.

[81] 12 U.S.C. §5371.

[82] Federal Reserve, OCC, "Regulatory Capital Rules," 78 Federal Register 62020, October 11, 2013. For more information, see CRS Report R42744, *U.S. Implementation of the Basel Capital Regulatory Framework*, by Darryl E. Getter.

[83] Federal Reserve, "Small Bank Holding Company Policy Statement," 80 *Federal Register* 20153, April 15, 2015, at https://www.gpo.gov/fdsys/pkg/FR-2015-04-15/pdf/2015-08513.pdf.

[84] This section was authored by Sean Hoskins, analyst in Financial Economics.

[85] Under 12 U.S.C. § 1467a(m), federal savings associations are subject to a qualified thrift lender test that requires thrifts to hold qualified thrift investments.

[86] 12 U.S.C. §1464(c)(2).

[87] For a comparison of the powers of national banks and federal savings associations, see OCC, *Summary of the Powers of National Banks and Federal Savings Associations*, August 31, 2011, at http://www.occ.treas.gov/publications/ publications-by-type/other-publications-reports/pub-other-fsa-nb-powers-chart.pdf.

[88] Simon Kwan, *Bank Charters vs. Thrift Charters*, Federal Reserve Bank of San Francisco, April 24, 1998, at http://www.frbsf.org/economic-research/publications/economic-letter/1998/april/bank-charters-vs-thrift-charters/.

[89] OCC, *Conversions: Comptroller's Licensing Manual*, April 2010, at http://www.occ.treas.gov/publications/publications-by-type/licensing-manuals/conversi.pdf.

[90] ABA, *Expand the Flexibility of the Federal Savings Charter to Grow and Serve Communities*, at http://www.aba.com/Advocacy/Grassroots/Documents/HOLAFlexibility.pdf.

[91] Until 2010, thrifts were regulated by the Office of Thrift Supervision, which was abolished by the Dodd-Frank Act.

[92] H.R. 1660 §2.

[93] CRS Report R43167, *Policy Issues Related to Credit Union Lending*, by Darryl E. Getter.

[94] Credit Union National Association, *Letter in Opposition to* H.R. 1660, November 2, 2015, at http://royce.house.gov/ uploadedfiles/cuna_letter_on_hr_1660.pdf.

[95] This section was authored by Sean Hoskins, analyst in Financial Economics.

[96] 15 U.S.C. §§1601 et seq.

[97] CFPB, *Manufactured-housing consumer finance in the United States,* September 2014, p. 9, at http://files.consumerfinance.gov/f/201409_cfpb_report_manufactured-housing.pdf.

[98] According to the CFPB, about "three-fifths of manufactured-housing residents who own their home also own the land it is sited on." CFPB, *Manufactured-housing consumer finance in the United States,* September 2014, p. 6, at http://files.consumerfinance.gov/f/201409_cfpb_report_manufactured-housing.pdf.

[99] For more, see CFPB, *Manufactured-housing consumer finance in the United States,* September 2014, at http://files.consumerfinance.gov/f/201409_cfpb_report_manufactured-housing.pdf.

[100] P.L. 110-289.

[101] P.L. 111-203, §1401. The definition of mortgage originator has multiple exemptions, such as for those who perform primarily clerical or administrative tasks in support of a mortgage originator or those who engage in certain forms of seller financing.

[102] CFPB, *Manufactured-housing consumer finance in the United States,* September 2014, p. 51, at http://files.consumerfinance.gov/f/201409_cfpb_report_manufactured-housing.pdf.

[103] Rep. Stephen Fincher, *Congressional Record*, vol. 161, part 53 (April 14, 2015), p. H2178.

[104] Corporation for Enterprise Development, "Consumer Groups Sign On Letter Opposing H.R. 650," at http://cfed.org/ assets/pdfs/policy/federal/consumer_groups_sign_on_letter_opposing_HR_650.pdf.

[105] P.L. 103-325.

[106] CFPB, "High-Cost Mortgage and Homeownership Counseling Amendments to the Truth in Lending Act (Regulation Z) and Homeownership Counseling Amendments to the Real Estate Settlement Procedures Act (Regulation X)," 78 *Federal Register* 6855, January 31, 2013.

[107] Ibid, 6856.

[108] 12 C.F.R. §1026.34.

[109] In addition to the APR test and points and fees test, a mortgage can be high cost if there is a prepayment penalty that meets certain criteria, although that issue is not addressed by H.R. 650. See Ibid.

[110] 15 U.S.C. §1602(bb). Other thresholds apply to junior liens.

[111] In some cases, a point may be eXcluded from the definition of points and fees if the point results in a reduction in the interest rate that is charged to the borrower. See P.L. 111-203, §1412.

[112] 15 U.S.C. §1602(bb).

[113] Consumer Financial Protection Bureau (CFPB), *Manufactured-housing consumer finance in the United States,* September 2014, pp. 35-36, at http://files.consumerfinance.gov/f/201409_cfpb_report_manufactured-housing.pdf.

[114] CFPB, *Manufactured-housing consumer finance in the United States,* September 2014, p. 48, at http://files.consumerfinance.gov/f/201409_cfpb_report_manufactured-housing.pdf.

[115] Ibid, p. 48.

[116] Ibid, p. 30.

[117] Ibid, p. 6.

[118] Manufactured Housing Institute, "The Preserving Access to Manufactured Housing Act (S. 682/H.R. 650)," at http://www.manufacturedhousing.org/webdocs/S%20682%20HR%20650%20leave%20behind%20use.pdf.

[119] Executive Office of the President, Office of Management and Budget, *Statement of Administration Policy:* H.R. 650 - *Preserving Access to Manufactured Housing Act of 2015*, April 13, 2015, at https://www.whitehouse.gov/sites/ default/files/omb/legislative/sap/114/ saphr650r_20150413.pdf.

[120] Ibid.

[121] CBO, *Cost Estimate of* H.R. 650, April 3, 2015, at http://www.cbo.gov/sites/default/files/ cbofiles/attachments/ hr_650.pdf.

[122] This section was authored by Sean Hoskins, analyst in Financial Economics.

[123] CFPB, "Ability-to-Repay and Qualified Mortgage Standards Under the Truth in Lending Act," 78 *Federal Register* 6407, January 30, 2013. For more on the rule, see CRS Report R43081, *The Ability-to-Repay Rule: Possible Effects of the Qualified Mortgage Definition on Credit Availability and Other Selected Issues*, by Sean M. Hoskins.

[124] For the definition of a QM, see 12 C.F.R. §1026.43.

[125] CFPB, Prepared remarks of Richard Cordray at a meeting of the Credit Union National Association, February 27, 2013, at http://www.consumerfinance.gov/speeches/prepared-remarks-of-richard-cordray-at-a-meeting-of-the-creditunion-national-association/. For a preliminary analysis of the effect of the QM rule on originations, see Bing Bai, *Data show surprisingly little impact of new mortgage rules*, Urban Institute, August 21, 2014, at http://www.urban.org/ urban-wire/data-show-surprisingly-little-impact-new-mortgage-rules.

[126] It is possible, however, that the market may adapt and have new fees so that the current definition may not affect future outcomes.

[127] CFPB, "Ability-to-Repay and Qualified Mortgage Standards Under the Truth in Lending Act," 78 *Federal Register* 6587, January 30, 2013.

[128] In some cases, a point may be eXcluded from the definition of points and fees if the point results in a reduction in the interest rate that is charged to the borrower. See P.L. 111-203, §1412.

[129] 15 U.S.C. §1602(bb).

[130] An affiliated business arrangement is "an arrangement in which (A) a person who is in a position to refer business incident to or a part of a real estate settlement service involving a federally related mortgage loan, or an associate of such person, has either an affiliate relationship with or a direct or beneficial ownership interest of more than 1 percent in a provider of settlement services; and (B) either of such persons directly or indirectly refers such business to that provider or affirmatively influences the selection of that provider." See 12 U.S.C. §2602(7).

[131] CFPB, "Ability-to-Repay and Qualified Mortgage Standards Under the Truth in Lending Act," 78 *Federal Register* 6439, January 30, 2013.

[132] Federal Reserve Board, "A Consumer's Guide to Mortgage Refinancings," at http://www.federalreserve.gov/pubs/ refinancings/.

[133] CFPB, "Ability-to-Repay and Qualified Mortgage Standards Under the Truth in Lending Act," 78 *Federal Register* 6562, January 30, 2013.

[134] Letter from Mortgage Bankers Association, April 13, 2015, at http://mba.informz.net/MBA/data/images/HR685Leadership4132015.pdf.

[135] Ibid.

[136] The Realty Alliance, "Congress Should Pass the Mortgage Choice Act," at http://www.therealtyalliance.com/getpublicfile.asp?ref=41.

[137] 12 U.S.C. §§2601 et seq.

[138] CFPB, "Ability-to-Repay and Qualified Mortgage Standards Under the Truth in Lending Act," 78 *Federal Register* 6438, January 30, 2013.

[139] Executive Office of the President, Office of Management and Budget, *Statement of Administration Policy:* H.R. 685 – *Mortgage Choice Act of 2015*, April 13, 2015, at https://www.whitehouse.gov/sites/default/files/omb/legislative/sap/114/saphr685r_20150413.pdf.

[140] Ibid.

[141] Center for Responsible Lending, "H.R. 685 Will Lead to Higher Fees for Homebuyers," at http://ourfinancialsecurity.org/blogs/wp-content/ourfinancialsecurity.org/uploads/2015/04/hr685_will_lead_to_higher_fees_for_homebuyers-fact-sheet-3.18.15.pdf.

[142] CFPB, "Ability-to-Repay and Qualified Mortgage Standards Under the Truth in Lending Act," 78 *Federal Register* 6439, January 30, 2013.

[143] An *escrow* account is an account that a "mortgage lender may set up to pay certain recurring property-related expense ... such as property taxes and homeowner's insurance." Property taxes and homeowner's insurance are often lump-sum payments owed annually or semiannually. See CFPB, "What is an escrow or impound account?," at http://www.consumerfinance.gov/askcfpb/140/what-is-an-escrow-or-impound-account.html.

[144] The Realty Alliance, "Congress Should Pass the Mortgage Choice Act," at http://www.therealtyalliance.com/ getpublicfile.asp?ref=41.

[145] CBO, *Cost Estimate of* H.R. 685, April 3, 2015, at https://www.cbo.gov/sites/default/files/cbofiles/attachments/ hr_685.pdf.

[146] This section was authored by Sean Hoskins, analyst in Financial Economics.

[147] See 12 C.F.R. §1026.43 and see CRS Report R43081, *The Ability-to-Repay Rule: Possible Effects of the Qualified Mortgage Definition on Credit Availability and Other Selected Issues*, by Sean M. Hoskins.

[148] The CFPB originally defined small for the purpose of the ATR rule as having less than or equal to $2 billion in assets and originating 500 or fewer mortgages in the previous year. The September 2015 rule, among other things, raised the threshold to 2,000 mortgage loans. See CFPB, "CFPB Finalizes Rule to Facilitate Access to Credit in Rural and Underserved Areas," September 21, 2015, at http://www.consumerfinance.gov/newsroom/cfpb-finalizes-rule-tofacilitate-access-to-credit-in-rural-and-underserved-areas/.

[149] For the definition of rural, see 12 C.F.R. §1026.35.

[150] CFPB, "Ability-to-Repay and Qualified Mortgage Standards Under the Truth in Lending Act," 78 *Federal Register* 6543, January 30, 2013.

[151] CFPB, "Ability-to-Repay and Qualified Mortgage Standards Under the Truth in Lending Act," p. 6, at http://files.consumerfinance.gov/f/201305_cfpb_final-rule_atr-concurrent-final-rule.pdf.

[152] CFPB, "CFPB Finalizes Rule to Facilitate Access to Credit in Rural and Underserved Areas," September 21, 2015, at http://www.consumerfinance.gov/newsroom/cfpb-finalizes-rule-to-facilitate-access-to-credit-in-rural-andunderserved-areas/.

[153] CFPB, "Amendments Relating to Small Creditors and Rural or Underserved Areas Under the Truth in Lending Act (Regulation Z)," p. 73, at http://files.consumerfinance.gov/f/201509_cfpb_amendments-relating-to-small-creditors-andrural-or-underserved-areas-under-the-truth-in-lending-act-regulation-z.pdf.

[154] Ibid, p. 76

[155] Ibid, p. 77.

[156] Ibid, p. 77.

[157] Rep. Andy Barr, *Congressional Record*, vol. 161, part 52 (April 13, 2015), p. H2121.

[158] Conference of State Bank Supervisors, "Letter of Support for H.R. 2672," December 4, 2013, at http://www.csbs.org/legislative/Documents/CSBSLetterofSupportforHR2672Dec42013.pdf.

[159] Rep. Andy Barr, *Congressional Record*, vol. 161, part 52 (April 13, 2015), p. H2121.

[160] CBO, *Cost Estimate of* H.R. 1259, April 6, 2015, at https://www.cbo.gov/sites/default/files/cbofiles/attachments/hr1259.pdf.

[161] This section was authored by Sean Hoskins, analyst in Financial Economics.

[162] A similar bill, H.R. 4521, was ordered to be reported by the Financial Services Committee in the 113th Congress.

[163] CFPB, "What is an escrow or impound account?," at http://www.consumerfinance.gov/askcfpb/140/what-is-anescrow-or-impound-account.html.

[164] A higher-priced mortgage loan is different from a high-cost mortgage described in H.R. 650. (See "Manufactured Housing.")

[165] The average prime offer rate (APOR) is an estimate of the market mortgage rate based on a survey of rates. The CFPB will publish the APOR weekly.

[166] CFPB, "Escrow Requirements Under the Truth in Lending Act (Regulation Z)," 78 *Federal Register* 4726, January 22, 2013.

[167] See CRS Report RS22172, *The Conforming Loan Limit*, by N. Eric Weiss and Sean M. Hoskins.

[168] CFPB, *Small Entity Compliance Guide: TILA Escrow Rule,* April 18, 2013, p. 4, at http://files.consumerfinance.gov/ f/201307_cfpb_updated-sticker_escrows-implementation-guide.pdf.

[169] P.L. 111-203, §1461.

[170] See 12 C.F.R. §1026.35 and CFPB, "Escrow Requirements Under the Truth in Lending Act (Regulation Z)," 78 *Federal Register* 4726, January 22, 2013. The CFPB's September 2015 rule also the escrow requirements, see CFPB, "Amendments Relating to Small Creditors and Rural or Underserved Areas Under the Truth in Lending Act (Regulation Z)," at http://files.consumerfinance.gov/f/201509_cfpb_amendments-relating-to-small-creditors-and-ruralor-underserved-areas-under-the-truth-in-lending-act-regulation-z.pdf.

[171] CFPB, "Escrow Requirements Under the Truth in Lending Act (Regulation Z)," 78 *Federal Register* 4747, January 22, 2013.The data the CFPB uses do not include non-depository institutions, so the CFPB estimates are a lower bound.

[172] Ibid., p. 4748.

[173] The CFPB expanded its definitions of small and rural, allowing more lenders to be deemed small and areas to be deemed rural. With this change, there would be more small lenders in rural areas than when the escrow rule was proposed in 2013, but H.R. 1529 would still increase the number of exempt lenders. See CFPB, "Amendments Relating to Small Creditors and Rural or Underserved Areas Under the Truth in Lending Act (Regulation Z)," at http://files.consumerfinance.gov/f/201509_cfpb_amendments-relating-to-small-creditors-and-rural-or-underservedareas-under-the-truth-in-lending-act-regulation-z.pdf.

[174] CQ Congressional Transcripts, "House Financial Services Committee Holds Markup on Financial Regulatory Legislation, March 25, 2015, at http://www.cq.com/doc/financial transcripts-4653577?9&search=M9QutUd4.

[175] Ibid.

[176] Ibid.

[177] Ibid.

[178] 12 U.S.C. §§2601 et seq.

[179] Some of the servicing requirements are specific mandates in the Dodd-Frank Act, and some are issued at the discretion of the CFPB pursuant to its authority under RESPA and TILA.

[180] CFPB, "Mortgage Servicing Rules Under the Real Estate Settlement Procedures Act (Regulation X)," 78 *Federal Register* 10695, February 14, 2013, and CFPB, "Mortgage Servicing Rules Under the Truth in Lending Act (Regulation Z)," 78 *Federal Register* 10901, February 14, 2013.

[181] See, for example, 12 C.F.R. 1026.41. The CFPB provided exemptions to small servicers from certain TILA requirements using its authority under TILA. The CFPB elected not to extend certain RESPA requirements to small servicers. See CFPB, "Mortgage Servicing Rules Under the Real Estate Settlement Procedures Act (Regulation X)," 78 *Federal Register* 10699, February 14, 2013.

[182] H.R. 4521, §3.

[183] For a full list, see 12 U.S.C. §2605 and CFPB, "Mortgage Servicing Rules Under the Real Estate Settlement Procedures Act (Regulation X)," 78 *Federal Register* 10699, February 14, 2013.

[184] CFPB, "Mortgage Servicing Rules Under the Truth in Lending Act (Regulation Z)," 78 *Federal Register* 10980, February 14, 2013.

[185] Ibid, p. 10980.

[186] Ibid, p. 10975.

[187] Ibid, p. 10981.

[188] Ibid, p. 10982.

[189] Ibid, p. 10981.

[190] Ibid, p. 10981. The CFPB notes that its estimates are only for depository institutions and do not include non-depositories due to data limitations.

[191] Attributed to Rep. Brad Sherman by CQ Congressional Transcripts, "House Financial Services Committee Holds Markup on Financial Regulatory Legislation," March 25, 2015, at http://www.cq.com/doc/financialtranscripts4653577?0&search=4xqeO9ST.

[192] Attributed to Rep. Blaine Luetkemeyer by CQ Congressional Transcripts, "House Financial Services Committee Holds Markup on Financial Regulatory Legislation," March 25, 2015, at http://www.cq.com/doc/financialtranscripts4653577?0&search=4xqeO9ST.

[193] Attributed to Rep. Maxine Waters by CQ Congressional Transcripts, "House Financial Services Committee Holds Markup on Financial Regulatory Legislation," March 25, 2015, at http://www.cq.com/doc/financialtranscripts4653577?0&search=4xqeO9ST.

[194] Ibid. See also CRS Report R41491, *"Robo-Signing" and Other Alleged Documentation Problems in Judicial and Nonjudicial Foreclosure Processes*, by David H. Carpenter.

[195] CBO, *Cost Estimate of* H.R. 1529, April 3, 2015, at https://www.cbo.gov/sites/default/files/cbofiles/attachments/ hr_1529.pdf.

[196] This section was authored by Sean Hoskins, analyst in Financial Economics.

[197] CFPB, "Ability-to-Repay and Qualified Mortgage Standards Under the Truth in Lending Act," 78 Federal Register 6416, January 30, 2013.

[198] A lender that originates a QM is entitled to a "presumption of compliance" with the ATR requirement, but the type of presumption of compliance and the amount of legal protection the lender receives depends on the mortgage interest rate. A QM with an annual percentage rate (APR) less than 1.5 percentage points above the average prime offer rate (APOR) for a first lien or less than 3.5 percentage points above the APOR for a subordinate lien qualifies for a *safe harbor*, a conclusive presumption of compliance with the ATR requirement. Mortgages that qualify for a safe harbor are referred to by the CFPB as *prime* mortgages. Mortgages above the thresholds that otherwise meet the QM requirements are deemed to be "higher-priced covered transactions" and qualify for a *rebuttable presumption* of compliance. The CFPB refers to QMs receiving a rebuttable presumption as *subprime* loans. See CFPB, "Ability-toRepay and Qualified Mortgage Standards Under the Truth in Lending Act," 78 *Federal Register* 6408, January 30, 2013.

[199] CFPB, Prepared remarks of Richard Cordray at a meeting of the Credit Union National Association, February 27, 2013, at http://www.consumerfinance.gov/speeches/prepared-remarks-of-richard-cordray-at-a-meeting-of-the-creditunion-national-association/. For a preliminary analysis of the effect of the QM rule on originations, see Bing Bai, Data show surprisingly little impact of new mortgage rules, Urban Institute, August 21, 2014, at http://www.urban.org/ urban-wire/data-show-surprisingly-little-impact-new-mortgage-rules.

[200] CFPB, "Ability-to-Repay and Qualified Mortgage Standards Under the Truth in Lending Act," p. 5, at http://files.consumerfinance.gov/f/201305_cfpb_final-rule_atr-concurrent-final-rule.pdf.

[201] The definition of "small" can be found in 12 C.F.R. §1026.35(b)(2)(iii)(B) and (C). The CFPB changed its definition of small from originating 500 mortgages in the previous calendar year to 2,000 mortgages. See CFPB, "Amendments Relating to Small Creditors and Rural or Underserved Areas Under the Truth in Lending Act (Regulation Z)," at http://files.consumerfinance.gov/f/201509_cfpb_amendments-relating-to-small-creditors-and-ruralor-underserved-areas-under-the-truth-in-lending-act-regulation-z.pdf.

[202] CFPB, "Ability-to-Repay and Qualified Mortgage Standards Under the Truth in Lending Act (Regulation Z)," 78 *Federal Register* 35431, June 12, 2013.

[203] CFPB, "Ability-to-Repay and Qualified Mortgage Standards Under the Truth in Lending Act (Regulation Z)," 78 *Federal Register* 6539, January 30, 2013.

[204] Ibid.

[205] CFPB, "Ability-to-Repay and Qualified Mortgage Standards Under the Truth in Lending Act (Regulation Z)," 78 *Federal Register* 35483, June 12, 2013.

[206] CFPB, "Ability-to-Repay and Qualified Mortgage Standards Under the Truth in Lending Act (Regulation Z)," 78 *Federal Register* 35437, June 12, 2013.

[207] Ibid.

[208] Congressional Budget Office (CBO), *Cost Estimate of* H.R. 1210, September 29, 2015, at https://www.cbo.gov/ sites/default/files/114th-congress-2015-2016/costestimate/hr1210.pdf.

[209] Congressional Budget Office (CBO), *Cost Estimate of* H.R. 1210, September 29, 2015, at https://www.cbo.gov/sites/default/files/114th-congress-2015-2016/costestimate/hr1210.pdf.

[210] Parts of this section were adapted from CRS Legal Sidebar WSLG1348, *Administrative Gaffe Forces CFPB to Delay Mortgage Disclosure Rule*, by David H. Carpenter.

[211] S. 1484, §117 (S. 1910, §918).

[212] S. 1484, §117 (S. 1910, §918).

[213] CFPB, "Integrated Mortgage Disclosures Under the Real Estate Settlement Procedures Act (Regulation X) and the Truth In Lending Act (Regulation Z)," 78 *Federal Register* 79730, December 31, 2013.

[214] CFPB, "Integrated Mortgage Disclosures Under the Real Estate Settlement Procedures Act (Regulation X) and the Truth In Lending Act (Regulation Z)," 78 *Federal Register* 79734, December 31, 2013.

[215] P.L. 111-203, §1100A.

[216] CFPB, "Know Before You Owe," at http://www.consumerfinance.gov/know-before-you-owe/.

[217] Lisa Prevost, "Request for Delay of Mortgage-Disclosure Rule," *The New York Times*, May 29, 2015, at http://www.nytimes.com/2015/05/31/realestate/request-for-delay-of-mortgage-disclosure-rule.html.

[218] Letter from industry groups to Richard Cordray, Director of the CFPB, March 18, 2015, at https://www.mba.org/ Documents/Comment%20Letters/03-18-15sign-onlettertoCFPBon TILA-RESPA.PDF.

[219] CFPB, "2013 Integrated Mortgage Disclosures Under RESPA and TILA; Delay of Effective Date," at http://files.consumerfinance.gov/f/201507_cfpb_2013-integrated-mortgage-disclosures-rule-under-the-real-estate-settlement-procedures-act-regulation-x-and-the-truth-in-lending-act-regulation-z-and-amendments-delay-of-effective-date.pdf.

[220] 5 U.S.C. §801 et seq.

[221] For the definition of *major rule,* see 5 U.S.C. §804.

[222] CFPB, "2013 Integrated Mortgage Disclosures Under RESPA and TILA; Delay of Effective Date," at http://files.consumerfinance.gov/f/201507_cfpb_2013-integrated-mortgage-disclosures-rule-under-the-real-estate-settlement-procedures-act-regulation-x-and-the-truth-in-lending-act-regulation-z-and-amendments-delay-of-effective-date.pdf.

[223] Trey Garrison, "Industry Welcomes TRID Grace Period But Congress Says It's Not Enough," *Housingwire*, June 3, 2015, at http://www.housingwire.com/articles/34086-industry-welcomes-trid-grace-period-but-congress-says-its-notenough.

[224] Letter from Richard Cordray, CFPB Director, to Rep. Barr and Maloney, June 3, 2015, at http://www.cfpbmonitor.com/files/2015/06/2015-06-03-RC-to-Barr-Maloney-et-al_TILA-RESPA.pdf. Also see, CFPB, "Know Before You Owe: You'll get 3 days to review your mortgage closing documents," June 3, 2015, at http://www.consumer finance.gov/blog/know-before-you-owe-youll-get-3-days-to-review-your-mortgage-closing-documents/.

[225] CFPB, "CFPB Sends Industry Letter on Know Before You Owe Mortgage Disclosure Rule Compliance," press release, October 2, 2015.

[226] Rep. Andy Barr, "Barr Responds to CFPB's New TRID Effective Date," press release, June 18, 2015, at https://barr.house.gov/media-center/press-releases/barr-responds-to-cfpb-s-new-trid-effective-date.

[227] Ibid.

[228] Mortgage Bankers Association, "TILA-RESPA Integrated Disclosure Rule," at https://www.mba.org/issues/ residential-issues/tila/respa-integration-rule.

[229] Attributed to Rep. Maxine Waters by CQ Congressional Transcripts, "House Financial Services Committee Holds Markup on Financial Services Bills, Day 1," July 28, 2015, at http://www.cq.com/doc/financialtranscripts-4736108?0.

[230] Ibid.

[231] Ibid.

[232] Letter from Consumer Groups to Members of Congress, July 27, 2015, at https://www.nclc.org/images/pdf/ legislation/letter-opposing-hr3192-2015.pdf.

[233] Congressional Budget Office (CBO), *Cost Estimate of* H.R. 3192, September 28, 2015, at https://www.cbo.gov/ sites/default/files/114th-congress-2015-2016/costestimate/hr3192.pdf.

[234] This section was authored by Marc Labonte, specialist in Macroeconomic Policy.

[235] U.S. Congress, House Committee on Financial Services, *Eliminate Privacy Notice Confusion Act*, report to accompany H.R. 601, 114th Cong., 1st sess., April 13, 2015, H.Rept. 114-59.

[236] For a summary of the requirement, see Federal Trade Commission, *In Brief: The Financial Privacy Requirements of the Gramm-Leach-Bliley Act*, July 2002, at https://www.ftc.gov/ tips-advice/business-center/guidance/brief-financialprivacy-requirements-gramm-leach-bliley-act.

[237] CFPB, 12 C.F.R. Part 1016, Docket No. CFPB–2014–0010, RIN 3170–AA39, p. 64059, at http://www.gpo.gov/fdsys/pkg/FR-2014-10-28/pdf/2014-25299.pdf; http://fsroundtable.org/hr-601-eliminate-privacy-notice-confusion-act/.

[238] CFPB, 12 C.F.R. Part 1016, Docket No. CFPB–2014–0010, RIN 3170–AA39, at http://www.gpo.gov/fdsys/pkg/FR2014-10-28/pdf/2014-25299.pdf.

[239] CBO, *Cost Estimate of* H.R. 601, April 7, 2015, at https://www.cbo.gov/sites/ default/files/cbofiles/attachments/ hr601.pdf.

[240] 12 C.F.R. §7.4000.

[241] This section was authored by Sean Hoskins, analyst in Financial Economics, and Marc Labonte, specialist in Macroeconomic Policy.

[242] CBO, *Cost Estimate for* H.R. 1553, September 10, 2015, https://www.cbo.gov/sites/ default/files/114th-congress2015-2016/costestimate/hr1553.pdf.

[243] For example, see Federal Reserve System, Inspection Frequency and Scope Requirements for Bank Holding Companies and Savings and Loan Holding Companies with Total Consolidated Assets of $10 Billion or Less, SR 13 21, December 17, 2013, at http://www.federalreserve.gov/bankinforeg/srletters/sr1321.htm.

[244] P.L. 109-351. For more information, see FFIEC, *Joint Report to Congress: EGRPRA*, July 31, 2007, p. 60, at http://egrpra.ffiec.gov/docs/egrpra-joint-report.pdf.

[245] CBO, *Cost Estimate for* H.R. 1553, September 10, 2015, https://www.cbo.gov/sites/default/files/114th-congress2015-2016/costestimate/hr1553.pdf.

[246] Gov. Daniel Tarullo, "A Tiered Approach to Regulation and Supervision of Community Banks," speech at the Community Bankers Symposium, Chicago, Illinois, November, 7, 2014, at http://www.federalreserve.gov/newsevents/ speech/tarullo20141107a.htm.

[247] U.S. Congress, Senate Committee on Banking, Housing, and Urban Affairs, *Testimony of Governor Daniel K. Tarullo, Federal Reserve*, 113th Cong., 2nd sess., September 9, 2014. More information on the pilot program is available at Federal Reserve System, "Federal Reserve Seeks to Conduct More Loan Reviews Off-Site," at https://www.community bankingconnections.org/articles/2014/q2/loan-reviews-off-site.

[248] Senior Deputy Comptroller Toney Bland, Testimony before the House Financial Services Committee, 114th Congress, April 23, 2015, at http://financialservices.house. gov/uploadedfiles/hhrg-114-ba15-wstate-tbland20150423.pdf.

[249] Department of the Treasury, Office of Inspector General, *Safety and Soundness: Review of OCC Community Bank Examination and Appeals Processes*, August 31, 2012, at http://www.treasury.gov/about/organizational-structure/ig/ Audit%20Reports%20and%20Testimonies/OIG12070.pdf.

[250] See FDIC, Office of Inspector General, *The FDIC's Examination Process for Small Community Banks*, AUD-12- 011, p. 8, August 2012, at http://www.fdicoig.gov/ reports12/12-011AUD.pdf.

[251] Federal Reserve System, Office of Inspector General, *Audit of the Small Community Bank Examination Process*, p. 18, August 2012, at http://oig.federalreserve.gov/reports/ Audit_SCB_Exam_Process_August2012.pdf.

[252] Data are for banks with high CAMELS rating. See FDIC Office of Inspector General, *The FDIC's Examination Process for Small Community Banks*, AUD-12-011, August 2012, at http://www.fdicoig.gov/reports12/12- 011AUD.pdf.
[253] This section was authored by Sean Hoskins, analyst in Financial Economics, and Marc Labonte, specialist in Macroeconomic Policy.
[254] The Federal Financial Institutions Examination Council (FFIEC) is an interagency council established by Congress to "prescribe uniform principles and standards for federal examination of financial institutions" and create standardized reporting forms. FFIEC consists of representatives from the OCC, Fed, FDIC, NCUA, CFPB, and a state regulator.
[255] 12 U.S.C. §4806.
[256] The CFPB only examines banks with over $10 billion in assets.
[257] See OCC, *OCC Bulletin 2013-15: Bank Appeals Process*, at http://www.occ.gov/news-issuances/bulletins/2013/ bulletin-2013-15.html.
[258] P.L. 103-325.
[259] P.L. 103-325, §309.
[260] Federal Reserve System, Office of Inspector General, *Audit of the Small Community Bank Examination Process*, August 2012, p. 23, at http://oig.federalreserve.gov/reports/Audit_SCB_Exam_Process_August2012.pdf.
[261] OCC, "Guidance for Bankers," June 7, 2013, at http://www.occ.gov/news-issuances/bulletins/2013/bulletin-2013- 15.html.
[262] 12 U.S.C. §4806.
[263] The ombudsman is explicitly funded by the regulators in S. 1494, but funding is not specified in H.R. 1941.
[264] American Bankers Association, "Examination Review/Appeals Process," webpage, http://www.aba.com/Issues/ Index/Pages/Issues_ExaminationReview.aspx.
[265] Department of the Treasury, Office of Inspector General, *Safety and Soundness: Review of OCC Community Bank Examination and Appeals Processes*, August 31, 2012, at http://www.treasury.gov/about/organizational-structure/ig/Audit%20Reports%20and%20Testimonies/OIG12070.pdf; FDIC, Office of Inspector General, *The FDIC's Examination Process for Small Community Banks*, AUD-12-011, August 2012, at http://www.fdicoig.gov/reports12/ 12-011AUD.pdf; Federal Reserve System, Office of Inspector General, *Audit of the Small Community Bank Examination Process*, August 2012, at http://oig.federalreserve.gov/reports/Audit_SCB_Exam_Process_August2012.pdf.
[266] This section was authored by Sean Hoskins, analyst in Financial Economics, and Marc Labonte, specialist in Macroeconomic Policy.
[267] Call reports can be accessed at https://cdr.ffiec.gov/public/.
[268] 12 U.S.C. §1817(a)(11).
[269] FFIEC, press release, September 8, 2015, http://www.ffiec.gov/press/pr090815.htm.
[270] Joint Agency, "Proposed Agency Information Collection Activities," 80 *Federal Register* 56539, September 18, 2015, http://www.ffiec.gov/press/PDF/2015xInitialF_%20Notice090715final.pdf.
[271] FFIEC, press release, September 8, 2015, http://www.ffiec.gov/press/pr090815.htm.
[272] 12 U.S.C. §§4805-4805a.
[273] U.S. Congress, Senate Committee on Banking, Housing, and Urban Affairs, *Testimony of Ms. Doreen R. Eberley,* FDIC, 113th Cong., 2nd sess., September 16, 2014.
[274] U.S. Congress, Senate Committee on Banking, Housing, and Urban Affairs, *Testimony of Ms. Doreen R. Eberley,* FDIC, 113th Cong., 2nd sess., September 16, 2014.

[275] American Bankers Association, "An Avalanche of Regulation," infographic, at http://www.aba.com/Issues/Index/ Documents/2014RegBurdenInfographic.pdf.

[276] Independent Community Bankers of America, *2014 ICBA Community Bank Call Report Burden Survey*, at http://www.icba.org/files/ICBASites/PDFs/2014CallReportSurvey Results.pdf.

[277] Parts of this section were adapted from CRS In Focus IF10031, *Introduction to Financial Services: The Consumer Financial Protection Bureau (CFPB)*, by David H. Carpenter and Sean M. Hoskins.

[278] Attributed to Senator Toomey by CQ Congressional Transcripts, "Senate Banking, Housing and Urban Affairs Committee Holds Markup on the Financial Regulatory Improvement Act," May 21, 2015, at http://www.cq.com/doc/ congressionaltranscripts-4691548?8 &search=Re1SwoJi.

[279] Attributed to Senator Brown by CQ Congressional Transcripts, "Senate Banking, Housing and Urban Affairs Committee Holds Markup on the Financial Regulatory Improvement Act," May 21, 2015, at http://www.cq.com/doc/congressionaltranscripts-4691548?8&search= Re1SwoJi.

[280] This section was written by Raj Gnanarajah, analyst in Financial Economics.

[281] For additional information see CRS Legal Sidebar WSLG1023, *FDIC Moves to Modify Guidance "Choking" Banking Services for Certain Legitimate Businesses*, by M. Maureen Murphy.

[282] The bill does not define "material reason," but states that it could be based on a banking regulator's belief that a specific customer or a group of customers pose a threat to national security, including any belief that they are involved in terrorist financing.

[283] U.S. Department of State, *State Sponsors of Terrorism*, at http://www.state.gov/j/ ct/list/c14151.htm.

[284] Congress frequently includes "reserve funds" in the budget resolution. Such provisions provide the chairs of the House or Senate Budget Committees the authority to adjust the budgetary allocations, aggregates, and levels included in the budget resolution in the future if certain conditions are met. Typically, these conditions consist of legislation dealing with a particular policy being reported by the appropriate committee or an amendment dealing with that policy being offered on the floor. Generally, the goal of such a reserve fund or adjustment is to allow certain policies to be considered on the floor without triggering a point of order for violating levels in the budget resolution. For a detailed description of reserve funds, see CRS Report R43535, *Provisions in the Bipartisan Budget Act of 2013 as an Alternative to a Traditional Budget Resolution*, by Megan S. Lynch.

[285] G. Bradley Weinsheimer, *OPR Inquiry Regarding Operation Choke Point*, U.S. Department of Justice - Office Of Professional Responsibility, July 7, 2015, p. 4.

[286] U.S. Congress, House Committee on the Judiciary, Subcommittee on Regulatory Reform, Commercial And Antitrust Law, *Guilty Until Proven Innocent? A Study of the Propriety and Legal Authority for the Justice Department's Operation Choke Point*, Statement of Stuart F. Delery, Assistant Attorney General Civil Division, 113th Cong., 2nd sess., July 17, 2014, pp. 1-3.

[287] Reportedly, Operation Choke Point was conceived in by the Department of Justice in 2012 and began in early 2013. Michael J. Bresnickat, *Justice News - Financial Fraud Enforcement Task Force*, The U.S. Department of Justice, March 20, 2013, at http://www.justice.gov/opa/speech/financial-fraud-enforcement-task-force-executive-directormichael-j-bresnick-exchequer.

[288] U.S. Congress, House Committee on the Judiciary, Subcommittee on Regulatory Reform, Commercial And Antitrust Law, *Guilty Until Proven Innocent? A Study of the Propriety and Legal Authority for the Justice Department's Operation Choke Point*, Statement of Stuart F. Delery, Assistant Attorney General Civil Division, 113th Cong., 2nd sess., July 17, 2014, pp. 1-2.

[289] U.S. Congress, House Committee on the Judiciary, Subcommittee on Regulatory Reform, Commercial And Antitrust Law, *Guilty Until Proven Innocent? A Study of the Propriety and Legal Authority for the Justice Department's Operation Choke Point*, Statement of Stuart F. Delery, Assistant Attorney General Civil Division, 113th Cong., 2nd sess., July 17, 2014, pp. 1-2.

[290] Federal Deposit Insurance Corporation, Office of Inspector General, *The FDIC's Role in Operation Chokepoint*, Report no. AUD-15-008, September 2015, p. iii, https://www.fdicig.gov/reports15%5C15-008AUD.pdf.

[291] U.S. Congress, House Committee on Oversight and Government Reform, *The Department of Justice's "Operations Choke Point": Illegally Choking Off Legitimate Businesses?*, Staff Report, 113th Cong., 2nd sess., May 29, 2014, pp. 1 8.

[292] Federal Deposit Insurance Corporation, Office of Inspector General, *The FDIC's Role in Operation Chokepoint*, Report no. AUD-15-008, September 2015, p. ii, https://www.fdicig.gov/reports15%5C15-008AUD.pdf.

[293] U.S. Congress, House Committee on Oversight and Government Reform, *The Department of Justice's "Operations Choke Point": Illegally Choking Off Legitimate Businesses?*, Staff Report, 113th Cong., 2nd sess., May 29, 2014, pp. 1 8.

[294] U.S. Congress, House Committee on Oversight and Government Reform, *The Department of Justice's "Operation Chokepoint": Illegally Choking Off Legitimate Businesses*, 113th Cong., 2nd sess., May 29, 2014.

[295] G. Bradley Weinsheimer, *OPR Inquiry Regarding Operation Choke Point*, U.S. Department of Justice - Office Of Professional Responsibility, July 7, 2015, pp. 4-5.

[296] Ibid, at 40-41.

[297] Ibid, at 41.

[298] Ibid. According to the review by the Department of Justice Office of Professional Responsibility, there was evidence that "that the attorneys had a legitimate reason for including such regulatory guidance."

[299] G. Bradley Weinsheimer, *OPR Inquiry Regarding Operation Choke Point*, U.S. Department of Justice - Office Of Professional Responsibility, July 7, 2015, pp. 4-5.

[300] Federal Deposit Insurance Corporation, Office of Inspector General, *The FDIC's Role in Operation Chokepoint*, Report no. AUD-15-008, September 2015, p. ii, https://www.fdicig.gov/reports15%5C15-008AUD.pdf.

[301] U.S. Congress, House Committee on Financial Services, Subcommittee on Oversight and Investigations, *The Federal Deposit Insurance Corporation's Role in Operation Choke Point*, Statement of Martin J. Gruenberg, 114th Cong., 1st sess., March 24, 2015, http://financialservices.house.gov/uploadedfiles/hhrg-114-ba09-wstate-mgruenberg-20150324.pdf.

[302] CBO, *Congressional Budget Office Cost Estimate* H.R. 766 *Financial Institution Customer Protection Act of 2015*, September 4, 2015, at https://www.cbo.gov/sites/default/files/114th-congress-2015-2016/costestimate/hr766.pdf.

[303] This section was authored by Gary Shorter, specialist in Financial Economics.

[304] P.L. 73-22.

[305] P.L. 112-106.

[306] This section largely derives from: Katherine Koops, "The JOBS Act and SEC Deregistration: New Thresholds and Special Considerations for Banks and Bank Holding Companies," *Bank Bryan Cave Law Firm*, June 8, 2012, at http://www.bankbryancave.com/2012/06/the-jobs-act-and-sec-deregistration-new-thresholds-and-specialconsiderations-for-banks-and-bank-holding-companies/.

[307] P.L. 73-291.

[308] See CRS Report R42572, *The Consumer Financial Protection Bureau (CFPB): A Legal Analysis*, by David H. Carpenter.

[309] See Independent Community Bankers of America (ICBA), "ICBA Statement on Senate Passage of JOBS Act," press release, March 22, 2012, at http://www.icba.org/news/newsreleasedetail.cfm?ItemNumber=123582.

[310] For example, see ICBA, "Key JOBS Act Provision Must Be Addressed to Benefit Thrifts," press release, September 13, 2012, at http://www.icba.org/files/ICBASites/PDFs/test091312.pdf.

[311] For example, see Jeff Blumenthal, "100-plus Banks Deregister Stock since JOBS Act," *Philadelphia Business Journal*, February 15, 2013, at http://www.bizjournals.com/philadelphia/print-edition/2013/02/15/100-plus-banksderegister-stock-since.html; Brian Yurcan, "Small Banks Deregister in Droves Due to JOBS Act," *Bank Tech*, May 30, 2012, at http://www.banktech.com/compliance/small-banks-deregister-in-droves-due-to-jobs-act/d/d-id/1295425.

[312] Joshua Mitts, *Did the JOBS Act Benefit Community Banks? A Regression Discontinuity Study*, April 25, 2013, at http://papers.ssrn.com/sol3/papers.cfm?abstract_id=2233502.

[313] This section was written by Raj Gnanarajah, analyst in Financial Economics.

[314] P.L. 100-86.

[315] The discussion surrounding Mutual Holding Companies (MHC's) in this report are from the perspective of an MHC that has a bank as a subsidiary. U.S. Securities and Exchange Commission, *"Mutual-to-Stock" Conversions: Tips for Investors*, October 6, 2011, http://www.sec.gov/investor/pubs/mutualconversion.htm.

[316] The Securities and Exchange Commission, *Mutual to Stock Conversions: Tips for Investors*, October 6, 2011, http://www.sec.gov/investor/pubs/mutualconversion.htm.

[317] The Office of Thrift Supervision ceased to exist as of 2011.

[318] Sec. 625 of P.L. 111-203, adding 12 U.S.C. §1467a(o)(11).

[319] The Board of Governors of the Federal Reserve System, "Savings and Loan Holding Companies," 76 *Federal Register* 56511-56513, September 2011.

[320] The Board of Governors of the Federal Reserve System, "Savings and Loan Holding Companies," 76 *Federal Register* 56508, 56521, September 2011.

[321] 12 U.S.C. §1467a(o)(11)(D).

[322] 12 C.F.R. §239.8(d)(4).

[323] Section 113 of S. 1484 refers to 12 C.F.R. §239.63 "or any successor thereto." The successor to 12 C.F.R. §239.63 is 12 C.F.R. §239.8(d).

[324] Federal Reserve Bank of St. Louis, *Order Approving Formation of a Holding Company and Acquisition of Nonbanking Subsidiaries - Northwest Bancorp, MHC.*, Federal Reserve Bulletin, December 1994, pp. 1131-1133.

[325] The Board of Governors of the Federal Reserve System, "Savings and Loan Holding Companies," 76 *Federal Register* 56512, September 2011.

[326] America's Mutual Holding Companies, *FAQ's America's Mutual Holding Companies*, http://www.americasmutualholdingcompanies.com/faq.html.

[327] Luse Gorman Pomerenk & Schick, Comments on Section 239.8(d) of Regulation MM of the Interim Final Rule Regarding Dividend Waivers by Mutual Holding Companies - Docket No. R-1429; RIN No. 7100 AD80, November 1, 2011, http://www.luselaw.com/publications/2011/ Ltr%20to%20FRB%20re%20public%20comments%20to%20Regulation%20MM%20%2800093534%29.PDF.

[328] Ibid.

[329] Federal Reserve, *Order Approving Formation of a Holding Company and Acquisition of Nonbanking Subsidiaries - Northwest Bancorp, MHC.*, Federal Reserve Bulletin, December 1994, pp. 1131-1133.

In: Bank Regulation
Editor: Miranda Schmidt
ISBN: 978-1-63485-520-4

Chapter 2

AN ANALYSIS OF THE REGULATORY BURDEN ON SMALL BANKS*

Sean M. Hoskins and Marc Labonte

SUMMARY

Since the financial crisis, policymakers have focused on addressing the failures that led to turmoil and ensuring that the financial system and the economy are better positioned to withstand future market disruptions. Some believe that the actions taken to realize these goals have been beneficial; others argue that the pendulum of regulation has swung too far and that the additional regulation has stymied economic growth and reduced consumers' access to credit. Much of the debate has centered on how new regulation has affected small banks.

A central question about the regulation of small banks is whether an appropriate tradeoff has been struck between the benefits and costs of regulation. The benefits of financial regulation include protecting consumers from fraud, discrimination, and abuse; ensuring that banks are less likely to fail; and promoting stability in the financial system. The costs associated with government regulation and its implementation is referred to as *regulatory burden*. The concept of regulatory burden can be contrasted with the phrase *unduly burdensome*, which refers to the relationship between benefits and costs. Some would consider a regulation to be unduly burdensome if costs exceed benefits or if the

* This is an edited, reformatted and augmented version of a Congressional Research Service, Publication No. R43999, dated April 22, 2015.

same benefits could be achieved at lower costs. The presence of regulatory burden does not mean that a regulation is unduly burdensome. Critics who believe that regulation is unduly burdensome point to the significant decline in the number of small banks over time. There could be other factors driving consolidation, however. For example, mergers are the largest cause of consolidation, and could occur when banks are financially strong or weak.

Of the 14 "major" rules issued by banking regulators pursuant to the Dodd-Frank Act (P.L. 111- 203), 13 either include an exemption for small banks or are tailored to reduce the cost for small banks to comply. In addition, during the rulemaking process, financial regulators are required to consider the effect of rules on small banks. Supervision and enforcement are also structured to pose less of a burden on small banks than larger banks, such as by requiring less frequent bank examinations for certain small banks. This report provides several examples that could be offered to counter views that there is a "one-size-fits-all" approach to bank regulation and that new regulation has increased regulatory burden relative to large banks. If small banks are facing unduly burdensome regulation, it is either in absolute terms or because small banks have less capacity for regulatory compliance than large banks do.

Quantifying the magnitude of regulatory burden has been a challenge for researchers because, among other reasons, federal statute does not require regulators to make quantitative estimates for all rules that they issue and because banks do not track the compliance costs spread throughout their operations. The difficulty in accurately assessing regulatory burden and in determining whether the burden rises to being unduly burdensome can make it challenging for policymakers to make informed judgments about the merits of proposals to provide regulatory relief.

The status quo is best characterized as applying ad hoc exemptions to certain regulations for banks based on their size and volume of activity, and most legislative proposals would adjust those exemption levels. Alternatives to the status quo range from regulating all banks in the same way, regardless of size, to implementing a separate regulatory regime for small and large banks, with various approaches in between. A focus on taxpayer protection and avoiding regulatory arbitrage would argue in favor of regulating all banks consistently. Rationales for regulating small banks differently from large banks include the systemic risk posed by large banks, economies of scale to regulatory compliance, a lack of critical mass of small banks to which some regulations would be relevant, and a desire by some policymakers to promote small banks.

INTRODUCTION

In response to vulnerabilities that had arisen during the financial crisis that began in 2007, Congress passed the Dodd-Frank Wall Street Reform and Consumer Protection Act[1] (Dodd-Frank Act) to strengthen financial stability and protect consumers. As the Dodd-Frank Act and other reforms have been implemented through recent rulemaking by financial regulators, some in Congress have claimed that the pendulum has swung too far. They argue that the additional regulation has resulted in significant regulatory burden, particularly for small banks, that has stymied economic growth and reduced consumers' access to credit. A frequently heard critique is that the regulations are "one-size-fits-all," and are unduly burdensome to small banks even though they were not the cause of the crisis. Those who are sympathetic to this argument believe that because large banks pose greater risks to the stability of the overall financial system, small banks should be exempted from regulations that might be useful or necessary for large banks.

Others, however, view the current regulatory structure as having achieved the appropriate tradeoff between the benefits and costs of regulation, and are concerned that regulatory relief for banks or other financial institutions could negatively affect consumers and market stability.

This report explains the concept of regulatory burden and the different ways it can be manifested. It analyzes whether small banks are *relatively* more burdened by regulation than big banks. To help answer that question, the report looks at the relative treatment of small and large banks in recent major regulatory proposals. It does not attempt to answer the question of whether small banks face too much or too little regulation in *absolute* terms, since that depends on policymakers' judgments about balancing financial stability, credit availability, consumer protection, and other objectives. The report also evaluates rationales for reducing the regulatory burden on small banks relative to large banks, policy approaches to do so, and the potential consequences on other market participants of providing relief to small banks.

What Is Regulatory Burden?

Financial regulation can result in both benefits and costs. The benefits of financial regulation— discussed in more detail in the section "Who Regulates Banks and What Do Regulators Do?"— include protecting consumers from fraud, discrimination, and abuse; ensuring that banks are less likely to fail; and promoting stability in the financial system. The cost associated with government regulation and its implementation is referred to as *regulatory burden*.

In the banking world, regulatory burden can be borne by banks, consumers, the government, and the economy at large. For example, under the Ability-to-Repay[2] requirement of the Dodd-Frank Act, a lender must verify that a borrower has the ability to repay a mortgage prior to offering the mortgage. The bank may face higher costs because it now must train its staff how to properly apply the rule and may spend more time reviewing each application. Some of this cost may be passed on to consumers through higher interest rates and fees or fewer lending options. The government may bear costs associated with writing rules to implement the statutory requirement and examining lenders to ensure that they are complying with the rules.[3] Regulatory burden could result in fewer mortgages being originated, which in turn could affect the broader economy through fewer home sales and reduced construction on new homes. The rule may have benefits— ensuring that borrowers are more likely to receive mortgages that they can repay—but there are also costs.

Regulatory burden on banks is manifested primarily in two different ways, operating costs and opportunity costs.[4] *Operating costs* (or *compliance costs*) are the costs the bank must bear in order to comply with regulation. For example, in response to a new rule, a bank may spend more money training its employees to ensure they understand the new rules, and the bank may have to purchase updated computer programs because the new rule defines concepts in ways that are incompatible with its old systems. Updating computer programs is an example of operating costs that are one-time costs borne upfront. Other costs, such as hiring additional compliance officers, are recurring costs that exist so long as the requirement is in effect. *Opportunity costs* are the costs associated with foregone business opportunities because of the additional regulation. A bank may, for example, offer fewer mortgages because new regulations make mortgage lending more expensive and instead choose to perform a different type of activity that is now more profitable.

Regulatory burden can influence where in the broader financial system a certain activity will be performed. Small-dollar loans, for example, can be offered by both banks and nonbank institutions (i.e., financial institutions that do not accept deposits), such as payday lenders. If a new regulation for small-dollar loans only applies to banks or it applies to both banks and nonbanks but it is less costly for nonbanks to comply, nonbanks would be expected to perform a larger share of small dollar loans. A comprehensive assessment of the broader societal costs and benefits of a regulation would need to include how the financial system adapts and responds to the regulation, which is beyond the scope of this report.

Much of this report focuses on the costs of regulation borne by banks. However, the presence of regulatory burden does not speak to the relationship between costs and benefits, and thus does not necessarily mean that a regulation is undesirable or should be repealed. A regulation can have benefits that could outweigh costs, but the presence of costs means, tautologically, that all regulations result in regulatory burden.

Regulatory Burden Versus Unduly Burdensome

The concept of *regulatory burden* can be contrasted with the phrase *unduly burdensome*. Whereas regulatory burden is about the costs associated with a regulation, unduly burdensome refers to the relationship between the benefits and costs of a regulation. All regulations result in regulatory burden, but policymakers are divided over which regulations, if any, are unduly burdensome.

The concept of regulatory burden can be contrasted with the phrase *unduly burdensome*. Whereas regulatory burden generally refers to the costs associated with a regulation, unduly burdensome refers to the relationship between the benefits and costs of a regulation. For example, some would consider a regulation to be unduly burdensome if costs are in excess of benefits or if the same benefits could be achieved at lower costs. But the mere presence of regulatory burden does not mean that a regulation is unduly burdensome. Policymakers that advocate for providing banks with relief from a regulation often do so because they believe the regulation is unduly burdensome, not just because it imposes a regulatory burden. Critics of a relief proposal typically accept that the regulation causes regulatory burden, but would likely argue that the burden does not rise to the level of being unduly burdensome because the benefits of the regulation justify its implementation.

To provide the context necessary to understand the regulatory burden on small banks, the next two sections explain what is meant by small bank and describe how banks are regulated.

What Is a Small Bank?

The term *bank* can be used to mean different things by different people, but this report will use the term bank as it is used in federal regulatory policy. Banks are a subset of d*epository institutions*, which are issued specific business charters by their primary regulator that permit them to accept deposits.[5] There are separate charters for commercial banks, thrifts (also called savings and loans, savings associations, and savings banks), and credit unions.[6] A charter may be issued by a federal or state regulator. This report focuses on federal depository institutions that are not credit unions and refers to them collectively as banks, unless otherwise noted.

Banks are typically classified as small or large based on their total asset size (i.e., the value of the loans and securities they hold), but there is no standard, commonly accepted threshold for what asset size constitutes a small bank. Some researchers define small as $1 billion or less in assets, whereas others define it as $10 billion or less. The Federal Reserve defines community banks as those banks with less than $10 billion in assets.[7] Often, the term *community bank* is used as a synonym for small bank. The Office of the Comptroller of the Currency (OCC) defines community banks as generally having $1 billion or less in assets.[8] Others define community bank by combining size with a focus on relationship-based services, such as lending, with the local community. The Federal Deposit Insurance Corporation (FDIC) has a research definition of community banking organizations, which it defines as (1) banks with less than $1 billion in assets as long as the bank makes loans and takes deposits, does not hold a large share of foreign assets, and is not a specialty bank; or (2) banks with more than $1 billion in assets that meet certain criteria, such as having more than one-third of their assets in loans, core deposits equal to at least half of their assets, and a limited geographical presence.[9] By this definition, not all small banks are community banks, and not all community banks are small banks, although the two are closely related.[10] Typically, the size of the bank is measured at the depository subsidiary level. Counterintuitively, this definition means that some very large and complex financial institutions own subsidiaries that qualify as small banks. *This report will use the terms small bank and community bank loosely because there is no widely accepted definition.*

The terms small bank and community bank as commonly used encompasses a disparate group of institutions, varying in size, activities, and charter. Asset size is not the most intuitive concept to understand what is meant by a small bank. To provide some additional perspective on the size of small institutions, it is informative to look at the number of employees at institutions of different asset sizes. At the end of 2014, a bank with approximately

- $100 million in assets had, on average, 25 employees,[11]
- $1 billion in assets had, on average, 214 employees,[12] and
- $10 billion in assets had, on average, 1,173 employees.[13]

These estimates might be larger than what a lay person would think of as a small institution. Notably, the average number of employees at a bank with $10 billion in assets is more than double the Small Business Administration's research definition of a small business as having 500 employees or less.[14]

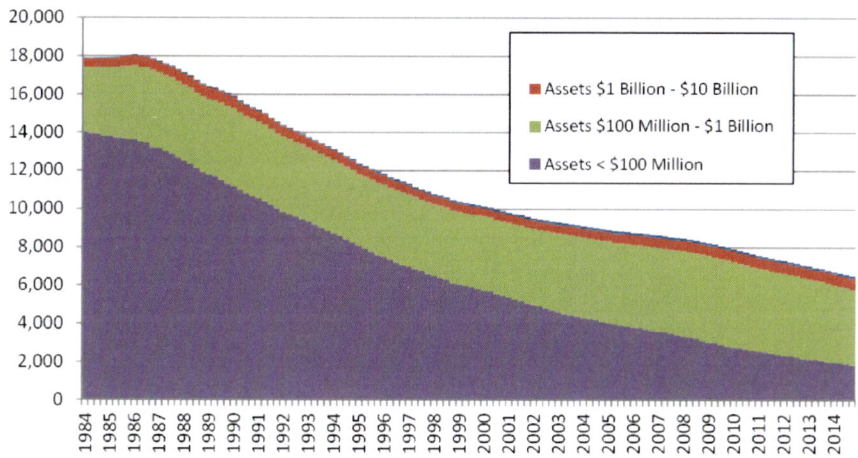

Source: Figure created by CRS using data from the FDIC.
Note: Banks with assets greater than $10 billion is the small blue line at the top of the graph.

Figure 1. Number of Banking Institutions, 1984-2014.

Small banks, under almost any common definition, have seen their numbers dwindle and their collective share of banking industry assets fall in recent decades. As **Figure 1** illustrates, there has been a long-term decline in the number of small banks in the United States, and, as shown in **Figure 2**, a long-term increase in the share of assets held by the largest banks. Overall, the number of institutions has fallen from a peak of 18,083 in 1986 to 6,509 in 2014. The number of banks with more than $10 billion in assets, shown in blue at the top of **Figure 1**, has nearly quadrupled in that time period, from 28 in

1984 to 107 in 2014. The number of banks with assets between $1 billion and $10 billion has been relatively stable over the past three decades, as has the number of banks with assets between $100 million and $1 billion. The most dramatic change has been in the number of banks with less than $100 million in assets, which has fallen from approximately 14,000 institutions in 1984 to 1,872 at the end of 2014.

The number of banks with more than $10 billion in assets has increased, as well as their share of total banking industry assets, from less than 30% in 1984 to more than 80% in 2014, as **Figure 2** shows. The share of industry assets held by the smaller categories of banks has decreased over that time period.

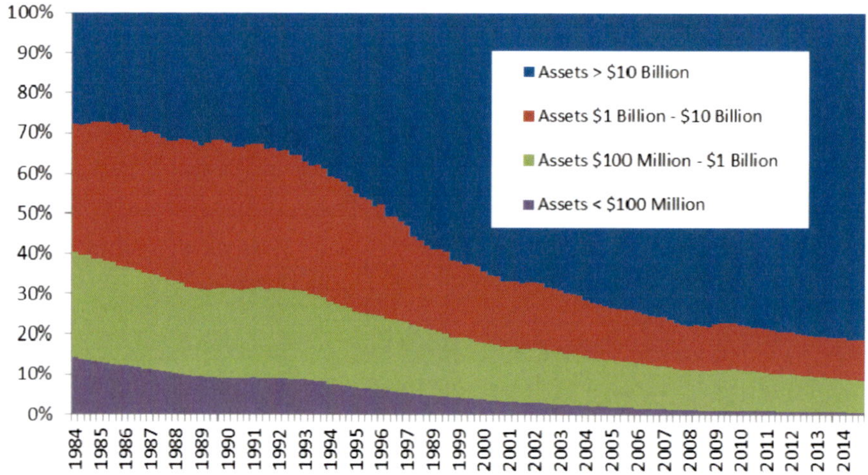

Source: Figure created by CRS using data from the FDIC.

Figure 2. Share of Industry Assets by Different Categories, 1984-2014.

The decrease in the number of banks from 9,904 in 2000 to 6,509 in 2014 has three main causes. Most of the decline in the number of institutions in that time period has been due to mergers (274 in 2014), as shown in **Figure 3**. Failures were minimal from 1999 to 2007, but played a larger role in the decline during the financial crisis and recession. As economic conditions have improved more recently, failures have declined (there were 18 in 2014). The number of "New Reporters," institutions providing information to the FDIC for the first time, has decreased in recent years and was zero in 2014 because there were no newly chartered banks.

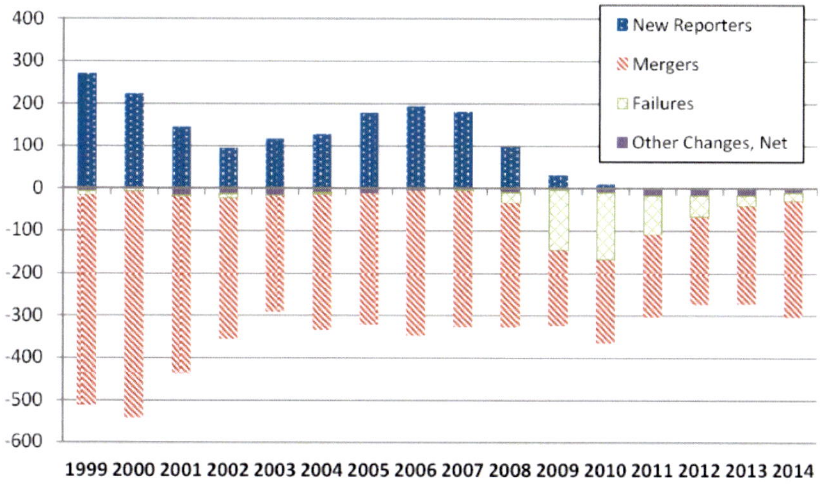

Source: Figure created by CRS using data from the FDIC.

Note: "Other Changes, Net" includes charter conversions, voluntary liquidations, adjustments for open-bank assistance transactions, and other changes.

Figure 3. Changes in the Number of FDIC-Insured Institutions, 1999-2014.

Some would take this industry consolidation to indicate that the regulatory burden on small banks has been onerous. Mergers—the largest factor in consolidation each year from 1999 to 2014— could take place from a position of strength or weakness, however. For example, a bank that is struggling financially may look to merge with a stronger bank in order to stay in business. Alternatively, a small bank that has been outperforming its peers may be bought by a larger bank that wants to benefit from its success. There are other fundamental changes in the banking system that are likely driving consolidation, making it difficult to isolate the effects of regulation.[15] First, the legal authority to bank across state lines was highly restricted through much of the twentieth century, and not entirely liberalized until 1997 as a result of the Riegle-Neal Interstate Banking and Branching Efficiency Act of 1994.[16] Second, there may be economies of scale (cost advantages due to size or volume of output) to banking, and they may be growing over time. For example, information technology has become more important in banking (e.g., cybersecurity and mobile banking), and certain information technology systems may be subject to economies of scale.[17] Third, the slow growth coming out of the most recent recession and macroeconomic conditions more generally, such as low interest rates, may make it less appealing for new entrants to enter the banking market. This report does not assess the extent to which industry consolidation is reflective of weakness in the financial performance of small banks, nor does it assess the financial status of small banks more broadly.

Who Regulates Banks and What Do Regulators Do?

The focus on regulatory burden in banking stems, in part, from the unique nature of banking regulation. As described in a CRS report, "Banking is one of the most heavily regulated businesses in the United States Nearly every aspect of the operation and management of an insured institution is subject to close regulatory supervision."[18] The Supreme Court once characterized the regulation of depository institutions as extending from an institution's cradle to its corporate grave.[19] Unlike the regulation of many other industries, supervision is carried out continuously and the statutes that banks must comply with cover a wider scope of policy areas, which will be discussed in this section.

To understand who regulates banks and how, it is important to consider what is meant by "regulation," broadly. Regulation can be thought of as having three distinct components: rulemaking, supervision, and enforcement.

1) *Rulemaking* refers to the process federal agencies follow to issue rules, pursuant to a grant of authority from Congress, and the end result of that process (i.e., the regulations that are issued).
2) *Supervision* refers to the power to examine banks, instruct banks to modify their behavior, and to impose reporting requirements on banks to ensure compliance with rules. In some cases, examiners confirm whether banks meet quantitative targets and thresholds set by regulation; in others, they have discretion to interpret whether a bank's actions satisfy the goals of a regulation.
3) *Enforcement* is the authority to take certain legal actions, such as imposing fines, against an institution that fails to comply with rules and laws.

Regulatory burden can occur through all three channels. For example, how much staff and resources are devoted to complying with a rule? How do banks' activities change when a new rule is adopted? How often should supervisory examinations occur and how long should they take? Do other banks adjust their behavior in response to an enforcement action against a peer?

In general, banking regulation can be thought of as divided into two main categories: (1) safety and soundness regulation and (2) consumer protection regulation.[20]

Safety and Soundness Regulation

Safety and soundness, or prudential, regulation is designed to ensure that a bank maintains profitability and avoids failure. To do so, regulators monitor the bank's risk profile and set various metrics that banks must maintain in areas such as capital and liquidity. Banks are assigned one of three prudential federal regulators based on their charter and corporate structure, as summarized in **Table 1**.

Table 1. Federal Prudential Regulators of Depositories

Primary Regulator	Banking Institutions Supervised
Federal Deposit Insurance Corporation (FDIC)	state banks that are not members of the FRS, state savings associations
Federal Reserve (Fed)	bank holding companies, state banks that are members of the FRS, savings and loan holding companies
Office of the Comptroller of the Currency (OCC)	national banking associations, federal savings associations
National Credit Union Administration (NCUA)	federally chartered or federally insured credit unions

Source: CRS based on 12 U.S.C. 1813(q)

Note: FRS = Federal Reserve System. This table does not include foreign banks or non-banks regulated by these agencies.

Different parts of the same banking organization may be overseen by different regulators, but each bank (or part of the bank) is assigned a primary federal regulator to reduce regulatory duplication. Jurisdictional overlap exists because of the historical evolution of the regulatory system. State banks are assigned a primary federal regulator, but are regulated at the state level as well. Credit unions are subject to a separate regulatory regime and are regulated by the National Credit Union Administration (NCUA). Differences in regulation between banks and credit unions are beyond the scope of this report.

Banks are federally regulated for safety and soundness for multiple reasons,[21] including ensuring that taxpayer funds, which ultimately back federal deposit insurance and the Fed's discount window, are safeguarded. Economists believe that access to a government backstop creates a moral hazard problem, meaning that federal backing gives a bank's creditors (such as depositors) less incentive to monitor the risks that the bank is taking. Prudential regulation can mitigate greater risk taking in the presence of moral hazard.

In principle, there is generally considered to be a short-run trade-off[22] between the safety and stability of banks and the cost and availability of bank credit. If regulation that is intended to make it less likely that a bank fails also increases the cost of offering loans and providing other services, a bank may reduce how much of its services it is willing to provide or consumers may be less willing to consume as much of the services because of the higher prices that could be passed on to them. It is also possible that additional prudential regulations that result in more costly services would result in activity migrating out of the relatively more regulated part of the financial system to less regulated parts of the system.[23]

Consumer Protection Regulation

Consumer protection focuses on ensuring that institutions conform to applicable consumer protection and fair-lending laws. Prior to the Dodd-Frank Act, the prudential banking regulators were charged with the two-pronged mandate of regulating both for safety and soundness and for consumer protection. Pursuant to the Dodd-Frank Act, the Consumer Financial Protection Bureau (CFPB)[24] acquired certain consumer protection powers over banks that vary based on whether a bank holds more or less than $10 billion in assets.

For banks with *more than $10 billion* in assets, the CFPB is the primary regulator for consumer protection, whereas safety and soundness regulation continues to be performed by the prudential regulator. As a regulator of larger banks, the CFPB has rulemaking, supervisory, and enforcement authorities. This means the CFPB can issue rules for a large bank to follow, examine the bank to ensure it is in compliance with these rules, and take enforcement actions (such as imposing fines) against banks that fail to comply. A large bank, therefore, has different regulators for consumer protection and safety and soundness.

For banks with *$10 billion or less* in assets, the rulemaking, supervisory, and enforcement authorities for consumer protection are divided between the

CFPB and the prudential regulators. The CFPB may issue rules that would apply to smaller banks from authorities granted under the federal consumer financial protection laws. The prudential regulator, however, would maintain primary supervisory and enforcement authority for consumer protection. The CFPB has limited supervisory authority over smaller banks; it can participate in examinations of smaller banks performed by the prudential regulator "on a sampling basis."[25] Although the CFPB does not have enforcement powers over small banks, it may refer potential enforcement actions against small banks to the banks' prudential regulators. (The prudential regulators must respond to such a referral but are not bound to take any other substantive steps.)

One of the long-standing issues in the regulation of consumer financial services is the perceived trade-off between protecting consumers and ensuring that providers of financial services are not unduly burdened. If regulation intended to protect consumers increases the cost of providing a financial product, a company may reduce how much of that product it is willing to provide and to whom it is willing to provide it. Those who still receive the product may benefit from the enhanced disclosure or added legal protections of the regulation but at the cost of a potentially higher price.

Other Forms of Regulation

In addition to safety and soundness regulation and consumer protection regulation, banks are also regulated for anti-money laundering, community reinvestment, as well as for a host of other things. The Treasury Department also issues some regulations with which banks must comply, such as economic sanctions. To the extent that banks participate in securities and derivatives markets, they are subject to activities-based regulations issued by the Securities Exchange Commission (SEC) and Commodity Futures Trading Commission (CFTC). Although there is regulatory burden associated with all of these areas, this report primarily addresses the regulatory burden associated with the activities of the banking regulators.

CHARACTERISTICS DETERMINING THE REGULATORY BURDEN A BANK FACES

Congressional debate on regulatory burden often emphasizes issues related to bank size, which will be discussed in detail in the rest of the report. Size is only one of several factors that influences burden, however. The regulatory burden borne by a bank depends on *what* rules are applied to it (rulemaking) and *how* those rules are applied (supervision and enforcement). The factors that determine what rules are applied and how include the following:

- **Charter**—Because a bank's primary regulator depends on its charter, to the extent that different bank regulators have different practices and policies, the charter will influence the regulatory burden. However, to reduce disparate treatment between regulators, the OCC, FDIC, and Fed often undertake joint rulemaking and participate in an interagency council, the Federal Financial Institutions Examination Council (FFIEC), established by Congress to "prescribe uniform principles and standards for federal examination of financial institutions" [26] and create standardized reporting forms. FFIEC consists of representatives from the OCC, Fed, FDIC, NCUA, CFPB, and a state regulator. State regulators can issue regulations that apply to state banks, as long as they do not conflict with federal law. State chartered banks have a state and primary federal regulator (either the FDIC or Fed). If the bank has a state charter, supervisory examinations can alternate between the state banking regulation and its primary federal regulator.[27] Differences in regulation and regulatory burden between banks and credit unions are a perennial concern of Congress, but beyond the scope of this report.
- **Risk profile**—Not all banks pose the same risk of failure, risk to consumers, and risk to the overall system, so policymakers tailor some regulations and supervisory practices by risk profile in order to reduce regulatory burden. For example, because small banks with higher supervisory ratings—signaling that they are perceived to be healthier—are, all else equal, less likely to fail, they are examined less frequently and intensely than banks with lower ratings.[28]
- **Business model**—Certain activities will attract more regulatory scrutiny than others because they are riskier, more complex, pose more risk to consumers or the broader economy, and so on. Different banks offer different types of services and engage in different types of activities; therefore, some banks will have greater regulatory compliance costs because they are involved in more activities or lines of businesses that require oversight. In other words, the same activity will require a certain amount of regulatory compliance at any bank that undertakes it, but some banks will undertake more of that activity

than others, which will result in proportionately more regulatory burden. Notably, if banks engage in certain activities, such as operating in the securities or derivatives market, it will trigger additional activity-based regulation.

The factors listed above can be correlated to different degrees with size. Size and *charter* are not closely correlated among the three federal bank regulators, in the sense that there is not a predominantly "big bank" or "small bank" regulator. Each is the primary regulator of at least 100 banks with more than $1 billion in assets and at least 700 banks with less than $1 billion in assets.[29] In absolute terms, the FDIC regulates the most banks over and under $1 billion in assets. Just as there are small and large banks regulated by each bank regulator, size is not the only factor determining whether to charter as a bank or credit union. Most credit unions are small, but there are also over 200 credit unions with more than $1 billion in assets, of which only 5 with more than $10 billion in assets. There is only one credit union with more than $50 billion in assets.[30]

It is difficult to draw any conclusions about the correlation between size and *risk profile* because information on supervisory ratings is confidential. Both small and large banks became financially distressed during and after the financial crisis. Looking at the correlation between size and measures such as capital ratios gives an incomplete picture of risk profile.

Size is somewhat correlated with *business model* in terms of the types of activities that large and small banks engage in. On average, small banks devote more of their activities to the traditional business model of taking deposits and making loans than large banks. The FDIC's definition of community bank can be used as a proxy for a traditional banking business model. As of the end of 2010, the FDIC found that 92 of 6,286 institutions with less than $1 billion in assets did not meet the FDIC's criteria of "community bank," which is defined in such a way that a certain percentage of the banks activities must be lending and deposit taking. By contrast, 298 of 628 institutions with more than $1 billion in assets did not meet the definition of community banks; these institutions held $11.3 trillion of $13.3 trillion in total industry assets.[31]

While there is no simple metric for determining the complexity of a bank's business model, a comparison of data from the bank holding company peer reports can be used as an example of the extent to large banks are more involved in more complex activities than small banks. For example, banks with less than $500 million in assets are less likely than banks with more than $10 billion in assets to have non-bank subsidiaries, such as broker-dealers, use derivatives, guarantee credit derivatives, have foreign activities, or fund themselves with other types of debt than deposits.[32]

Differences in How Small and Large Banks Are Regulated

As mentioned in the previous section, size is one of the factors that policymakers may consider in deciding whether to apply certain regulations to a bank and how a bank should be supervised. This section provides an overview of how small banks are regulated compared to larger banks.

Some argue that there is a one-size-fits-all model of regulation. One recent whitepaper opined, "The major flaw of the federal banking regulatory system is that it treats a community bank with $165 million in assets (the median-sized American bank) as the same essential creature as JP Morgan Chase or Bank of America."[33] Echoing a similar sentiment, Federal Reserve Governor Daniel Tarullo has described banking regulation as historically following a "unitary model," which he describes as a system where the broad principles underlying bank regulation are the same for all banks, regardless of their size and activities. A unitary approach to bank regulation was justified on the grounds that the basic rationale for safety and soundness regulation is to protect taxpayers in the presence of federal deposit insurance. In other words, the primary goal of regulation is to minimize the likelihood that a bank failure will require an infusion of federal dollars to make insured depositors whole, regardless of whether the bank is small or large.[34]

After the lessons learned from the financial crisis, however, Governor Tarullo argues that "the unitary approach of the pre-crisis period has been abandoned"[35] in the regulatory reforms of the last few years. He states that the Dodd-Frank Act and other reforms created "different categories of banking organizations—largely, but not exclusively, on the basis of total assets—to which different regulatory requirements are to apply."[36] Part of the rationale for establishing different categories of banks is the acknowledgment that, should larger banks fail, they do not just pose a risk to taxpayers through the deposit insurance fund but also jeopardize the stability of the broader financial system. Because the risks banks pose may differ by size, the regulation those banks face should also differ. Community banks, Governor Tarullo argues, "will suffer the fallout from systemic problems, [but] are unlikely to cause such problems" and their regulation should reflect their lower level of risk relative to large banks.[37] Governor Tarullo does not argue that the existing regulatory approach for small banks is perfectly tailored and even suggests specific regulations that he believes may be applied unnecessarily to small banks, such as the Volcker Rule.[38] But, in general, Governor Tarullo argues that recent reforms have largely differentiated between banks based on size and provided exemptions to smaller banks.

The following assesses the arguments made by Governor Tarullo and others who argue that small banks have been largely exempt from recent regulatory actions by analyzing whether rulemaking, supervision, and enforcement are different for small and large banks.

Rulemaking

Rulemaking can be thought of as having two major components: the *content* of a rule and the *process* of issuing a rule.[39] Congress may require or permit regulators to favor small banks, or regulators may choose to do so independently, in the content of any given rule on a case-by-case basis. Alternatively, Congress may require regulators to give small banks special consideration through the rulemaking process any time a new rule is issued.

For the content of rules, small banks may be differentiated from large banks in the rulemaking process primarily through exemptions and tailoring.[40] In an *exemption*, the rule does not apply to small banks under some specified numerical threshold, but it does apply to larger banks. An exemption for certain types of banks can be specified in statute or, in some cases, included at the discretion of the regulator or regulators issuing the rule. With *tailoring*, a rule may apply to small banks and larger banks, but the rule is structured to reduce the regulatory burden on small banks by, for example, offering streamlined compliance options. Tailoring may be recommended by Congress, but the details are often worked out by the regulators. Asset size is the most commonly used threshold, but other metrics, such as liabilities, deposits, or activity volume, are also used. For both exemptions and tailoring, different rules have thresholds at different asset sizes, such as $1 billion, $10 billion, $50 billion, and $250 billion, as discussed below.

Exemptions and tailoring are different approaches to reducing regulatory burden with each having its own strengths and weaknesses. Tailoring is used when policymakers want to make sure that a requirement still applies to small banks, but would like to reduce the burden associated with complying. Regulators may, for example, reduce the amount of paperwork that small banks have to report about the requirement. Not all regulations, however, are appropriate for—or well targeted to—small banks. In such instances, an exemption may be more effective at balancing the benefits and costs of regulation. In particular, some are concerned that regulators may initially tailor a regulation appropriately so that it targets small banks without being unduly burdensome, but over time there may be a trickle-down of the standards that are applied to larger banks by regulators or other market participants so that they are, in practice, applied to small banks. [41] Policymakers balance these tradeoffs in considering whether to include an exemption, tailoring, or neither in a regulation.

The next section provides several examples of long-standing regulations from which small banks have been exempted or received special tailoring. The following section ("Exemptions and Tailoring for Small Banks in Recent Rulemakings") explains how small banks have been affected by more recent regulations. The section after that ("Special Consideration in Statute for Small Banks in the Rulemaking Process") explains the different ways that small banks receive special consideration in the rulemaking process.

Examples of Longstanding Exemptions and Tailoring for Small Banks in Rules

Although many recent rules have exempted small banks (as discussed in the next section), adjusting rules based on size is not a new concept. Prior to recent financial reforms, small banks received exemptions from or special treatment for certain rules. For example, the Federal Reserve's Small Bank Holding Company Policy Statement allows bank holding companies with less than $1 billion in assets that meet certain criteria to hold more debt at the holding company level than capital requirements would otherwise permit if the debt is used for acquisitions.[42] This policy is motivated by recognition of differences between how small and large banks typically finance acquisitions. The policy statement is also, more recently, referenced in the "Collins Amendment" (Section 171) to the Dodd-Frank Act (P.L. 111-203) and the capital rule implementing Basel III.[43]

In addition, reserve requirements are tailored in favor of small banks. Banks are required to hold cash reserves against their deposits[44] in their vaults or at the Federal Reserve. The percentage of reserves that banks are required to hold against deposits is graduated based on the amount of deposits they hold. In 2015, banks do not have to hold any reserves for their first $14.5 million in deposits; from $14.5 million to $103.6 million of deposits, banks are required to hold reserves equal to 3% of deposits; and for deposits over $103.6 million, banks are required to hold reserves equal to 10% of deposits. Because reserves earn little income, lower reserve requirements for small banks allow them to use relatively more of their deposits to finance more profitable activities.

As another example, banks with assets of less than $500 million or $1 billion, depending on the provision, are also exempted from FDIC regulations and provisions of the Sarbanes-Oxley Act of 2002 (in the case of publicly traded banks) subjecting banks to certain corporate governance requirements pertaining to independent auditing, financial reporting, and internal controls. Exemptions were provided from some of these requirements because of concerns about regulatory burden.[45]

These examples illustrate that, even though some have characterized the past regulation of banks as following a unitary model, rules with exemptions and tailoring based on the size of the institution have long existed. Arguably, what has changed recently is that exemptions and tailoring are being applied with greater frequency. It is an open question whether the exemptions from more recent rulemakings, described in the next section, are best characterized as a continuation of a previous trend of altering regulations based on size or as a paradigm shift that has resulted in the abandonment of the unitary regulatory approach altogether.

Exemptions and Tailoring for Small Banks in Recent Rulemakings

An evaluation of how small banks have been affected by new rulemaking in recent years is hindered by both the sheer number of new rules and the fact that the effects of rules cannot easily be compared or aggregated, because some rules have large effects on banks and others have small effects. Therefore, this section focuses on "major rules" issued by banking regulators so as to highlight how those rules that are expected to have the largest effect are applied to small banks. A major rule is a rule that

> has resulted in or is likely to result in – (A) an annual effect on the economy of $100,000,000 or more; (B) a major increase in costs or prices for consumers, individual industries, Federal, State, or local government agencies, or geographic regions; or (C) significant adverse effects on competition, employment, investment, productivity, innovation, or on the ability of United States-based enterprises to compete with foreign-based enterprises in domestic and export markets.[46]

Using GAO data,[47] CRS identified 14 major rules that have been issued since 2010 pursuant to the Dodd-Frank Act and the Basel Accords. **Table 2** describes how each of these major rules affects small banks. Of the 14 major rules, 13 have either an exemption or are tailored for small banks. Prudential regulators (OCC, Fed, or FDIC) issued nine of the major rules and the CFPB issued five.

Table 2. Treatment of Small Banks in Recent "Major Rules" Issued by Banking Regulators Pursuant to the Dodd-Frank Act or the Basel Accords

Official Title	RIN	Differential Treatment of Small Banks
	Prudential Regulators	
(1) Liquidity Coverage Ratio: Liquidity Risk Measurement Standards	1557-AD74	Does not apply to banks with less than $50 billion in total assets.
(2) Regulatory Capital Rules: Regulatory Capital, Revisions to the Supplementary Leverage Ratio	1557-AD74	Does not apply to banks with less than $250 billion in total consolidated assets or $10 billion in total on-balance sheet foreign exposure.
(3) Prohibitions and Restrictions on Proprietary Trading and Certain Interests in, and Relationships With, Hedge Funds and Private Equity Funds ("Volcker Rule")	7100-AD82	Applies to all banks, but streamlined compliance policies and procedures for banks with less than $10 billion in assets.
(4) Treatment Of Certain Collateralized Debt Obligations Backed Primarily By Trust Preferred Securities With Regard To Prohibitions And Restrictions On Certain Interests In, And Relationships With, Hedge Funds And Private Equity Funds	1557-AD79	Applies to all banks that hold CDO-TruPs, including small banks.
(5) Regulatory Capital Rules: Regulatory Capital, Implementation Of Basel III, Capital Adequacy, Transition Provisions, Prompt Corrective Action, Standardized Approach For Risk-Weighted Assets, Market Discipline And	1557-AD46, 3064-AD95[a]	Does not apply at the holding company level to BHCs with less than $1 billion in assets. For banks with $15 billion or less in assets, the preferential capital treatment of trust preferred securities is grandfathered.

Official Title	RIN	Differential Treatment of Small Banks
Disclosure Requirements, Advanced Approaches Risk-Based Capital Rule, And Market Risk Capital Rule		Banks with less than $250 billion in total assets or $10 billion in foreign exposure are allowed an additional year to phase in the rule and are exempted from the rule's supplemental leverage ratio, advanced approaches for risk-weighted assets, and countercyclical capital buffer, and may opt out of the requirement that unrealized gains and losses be included in net income. Applies the "Market Risk rule" to thrifts with trading assets exceeding $1billion or 10% of consolidated assets.
(6) Risk-Based Capital Guidelines: Market Risk	1557-AC99	Does not apply to banks with aggregated trading assets and trading liabilities less than $1 billion or 10% of total assets.
(7) Debit Card Interchange Fees And Routing	7100-AD63	Does not apply to banks that do not issue debit cards. Does not apply to issuers that, together with affiliates, have $10 billion or less in assets.
(8) Enhanced Prudential Standards For Bank Holding Companies And Foreign Banking Organizations	7100-AD86	Does not apply to banks with less than $10 billion in assets. Most provisions do not apply to banks with less than $50 billion in assets.
(9) Supervision And Regulation Assessments For Bank Holding Companies And Savings And Loan Holding Companies With Total Consolidated Assets Of $50 Billion Or More And Nonbank Financial Companies Supervised By The Federal Reserve	7100-AD95	Does not apply to banks with less than $50 billion in assets.
Consumer Financial Protection Bureau		
(10) Ability-To-Repay And Qualified Mortgage Standards Under The Truth In Lending Act (Regulation Z)	3170-AA17	Applies to companies, including small banks, that extend mortgage credit but has additional compliance options—and more lenient thresholds—for certain additional legal protections for some small banks.

Table 2. (Continued)

Official Title	RIN	Differential Treatment of Small Banks
		Small is defined as having less than or equal to $2 billion in assets and originating 500 or fewer mortgages in the previous year.[c]
(11) Electronic Fund Transfers (Regulation E)	3170-AA15	Applies to companies, including small banks, that consistently send more than 100 remittances a year. Entities that send 100 or fewer remittances are not considered remittance transfer providers and are not covered by the rule.
(12) Loan Originator Compensation Requirements Under the Truth In Lending Act (Regulation Z)	3170-AA13	Applies to companies, including small banks, that originate mortgages, with a limited exemption from some requirements for originators that originate 10 or fewer loans in a 12-month period.
(13) Mortgage Servicing Rules Under the Real Estate Settlement Procedures Act (Regulation X)	3170-AA14	Applies to companies, including small banks, that service mortgages, but is adjusted for all companies that are deemed small servicers. A small servicer services 5,000 or fewer mortgages loans and only services mortgages that it or an affiliate originates. Small servicers are exempted from those parts of the rule established at the discretion of the CFPB, but must comply with those parts mandated by the Dodd-Frank Act.
(14) Mortgage Servicing Rules Under the Truth In Lending Act (Regulation Z)	3170-AA14	Applies to companies, including small banks, that service mortgages, but small servicers are exempted from certain requirements related to disclosures and periodic statements. A small servicer services 5,000 or fewer mortgages loans and only services mortgages that it or an affiliate originates.

Source: CRS analysis of major rules identified by GAO, "Congressional Review Act Resources," at http://www.gao.gov/legal/congressact/congress.html.

Notes: RIN = "Regulation Identifier Number." Hyperlink on Subject column leads to GAO description of rule. Hyperlink on RIN number column leads to rule as published in *Federal Register*. In some cases, the primary regulator has the discretion to exclude or include banks that otherwise would not meet the criteria listed above. The use of the term *banks* in this table refers to any type of depository subsidiary or depository holding company unless otherwise noted. For purposes of this table, prudential regulators are OCC, FDIC, and Fed, issuing rules alone or jointly with each other or other regulators. Some rules have multiple RIN numbers, which are not listed.

[a] CRS has combined two rules issued separately by regulators on separate dates that are substantively the same.

[b] There is currently a proposed rule to increase the threshold for the Small Bank Holding Company Policy Statement from $500 million to $1 billion.

[c] The CFPB recently issued a proposed rule to increase the threshold from 500 to 2,000 mortgages. See CFPB, "Amendments Relating to Small Creditors and Rural or Underserved Areas Under the Truth in Lending Act (Regulation Z)," 80 *Federal Register* 7769, February 11, 2015.

As can be seen in **Table 2**, recent regulations have not used a consistent qualitative or quantitative measure for determining exemptions or tailoring. Many rules use asset size, but some use number of activities (e.g., #11, the *Electronic Fund Transfers* rule). Even rules aimed at addressing the same policy issue use different thresholds—for example, rules aimed at policy issues posed by large, complex banks vary the exemption level between $10 billion, $50 billion, and $250 billion.

Most of the major rules issued by prudential bank regulators in **Table 2** are not focused on small banks but are geared primarily toward larger banks. This includes one of the major initiatives in the Dodd-Frank Act (Title I)—a new enhanced prudential regime applied only to banks with assets over $50 billion and non-banks that have been designated as systemically important (implemented through rules #8 and #9 in **Table 2**). [48] Eight of the nine major rules have some form or tailoring or exemption for small banks. The only rule that does not have an exemption or tailoring—#4, the *Treatment Of Certain Collateralized Debt Obligations Backed Primarily By Trust Preferred Securities*—modified the *Volcker Rule* to make it easier for banks to hold securities backed by a form of capital frequently issued by small banks.[49] Six of the eight major rules with either exemptions or tailoring have size threshold exemptions so that those rules will not apply to small banks at all. Of the remaining two rules, the *Volcker Rule* (#3) is tailored to reduce the compliance costs for banks with less than $10 billion in assets and small banks are subject to some of the *Basel III Regulatory Capital Rule* (#5), exempted from certain parts of the rule, received tailoring for certain provisions, and a delayed phase-in from the entire rule.

The five rules in **Table 2** issued by the CFPB only apply to those entities involved in certain activities. For example, the rules about originating mortgages (#10 and #12) generally apply to lenders who originate mortgages regardless of whether the entity is a bank. (The rules issued by prudential regulators, by contrast, apply to entities based on their charter, not the activities they perform.) Small banks would be exempt from CFPB rules, therefore, if they did not perform the activity covered by the rule. In addition, all five rules have some form of exemption or tailoring for small banks that perform the covered activity, though some of the exemptions and tailoring are rather limited. The two mortgage servicing rules (#13 and #14) have partial exemptions that are not based on the asset size of the bank but on the amount and type of servicing performed by the bank. The *Electronic Fund Transfers* rule (#11), which has to do with remittance transfers, and *Loan Originator Compensation Requirements* rule (#12) also have exemptions that are based on the amount of the activity performed by the bank, rather than asset size. The *Ability-To-Repay* rule (#10) is tailored to provide additional compliance options for small banks, with small defined based on the bank's asset size and the amount of the activity performed.

Table 2 is useful for understanding which major rules apply to small banks, but provides a limited perspective on recent rulemaking because many recent rules do not fit the criteria used in the table. The Dodd-Frank Act and the Basel Accords have resulted in other well-known rules besides those listed in the table that could still impose a regulatory burden on small banks but are not listed because they are not major rules. The table also does not include recent major rules that are not pursuant to the Dodd-Frank Act and the Basel Accords. Nor does the table include rules issued by the Treasury Department or securities and derivatives regulators which, in some cases, may also apply to small banks involved in those activities. **Table 2** is not intended to be an exhaustive list of all financial reform rules.

In addition to what is missing from the table, there are several points to keep in mind when assessing what is included in the table. The major rules listed in the table vary greatly in length, burden, and complexity; just counting up the number of rules that have been issued may be misleading about the likely effect on small banks. This is especially true given that some requirements may be divided into multiple major rules (e.g., the nine major rules issued by the prudential regulators cover four major policy initiatives)[50] and in other cases, multiple regulatory goals may be combined into a single major rule. Finally, the presence of an exemption or tailoring in a rule does not in and of itself mean that the rule is optimally structured to achieve its regulatory goal while simultaneously minimizing burden. The exemptions or tailoring included in a rule might apply to a relatively minor part of it. For example, although small banks are exempt from some parts of the *Basel III Regulatory Capital Rule* (#5), they are subject to many other parts of the rule that are viewed as significant. Even if an exemption or tailoring is initially structured to minimize burden, it is possible that the market may adapt and the burden could trickle down to small banks (one example is the possibility that the pricing restrictions on debit card issuers under $10 billion in assets from the *Debit Card Interchange Fees And Routing* rule (#7) may spread to small banks due to market forces).[51]

Special Consideration in Statute for Small Banks in the Rulemaking Process

Certain statutes require regulators to consider the regulatory burden on small banks when writing rules. For example, when promulgating new rules, 12 U.S.C. Section 4802 requires that "each Federal banking agency [the OCC, Board of Governors of the Federal Reserve System, and the FDIC] shall consider, consistent with the principles of safety and soundness and the public interest-(1) any administrative burdens that such regulations would place on depository institutions, *including small depository institutions* and customers of depository institutions.... " (emphasis added). Similarly, 12 U.S.C. Section 5512(b) states that the CFPB shall consider the impact of rules that it prescribes on banks and credit unions with less than $10 billion in assets. It also allows the CFPB to exempt providers of financial services (such as banks) from its rules based on total assets or the volume of transactions.

The requirement to consider costs and benefits does not necessarily mean the regulators are required to perform a quantitative cost-benefit analysis. Bank regulators are not subject to Executive Order 12866's requirement that agencies perform cost-benefit analysis, subject to the Office of Information and Regulatory Affairs's (OIRA's) review, for "economically significant" rules.

Pursuant to the Regulatory Flexibility Act (RFA; 5 U.S.C. §§601-612),[52] regulators are required to include in rulemakings an assessment of the rule's impact on "small entities," which would include—but is not limited to—small banks. Agencies are only required to make an assessment if they believe that the rule will have a "significant economic impact on a substantial number of small entities" (the terms *significant*, *substantial*, and *small* are not defined in the act). Since 2013, the banking agencies and CFPB have defined a small bank as assets of $500 million or less for purposes of the RFA, which is a lower threshold for small entities than the definition of small bank used by the FDIC, Fed, or OCC.[53] Most rules do not meet this statutory test.[54] Agencies can comply with the RFA by making a qualitative or quantitative assessment, and may waive this requirement under certain circumstances. If the rule is determined to have a significant economic impact on a substantial number of small entities, the regulator that is issuing the rule is required

> to describe, among other things, (1) the reasons why the regulatory action is being considered; (2) the small entities to which the proposed rule will apply and, where feasible, an estimate of their number; (3) the projected reporting, recordkeeping, and other compliance requirements of the proposed rule; and (4) any significant alternatives to the rule that would accomplish the statutory objectives while minimizing the impact on small entities.[55]

The CFPB, but not the other federal banking regulators, is required under the RFA to convene a small business review panel when a rule that it is developing may have a significant economic impact on a substantial number of small entities.[56] Through the review panel, the CFPB collects advice and recommendations from representatives who would be affected by the proposed rule related to, among other things, "any projected increase in the cost of credit for small entities" that may result from the rule and "any significant alternatives to the proposed rule which accomplish the stated objectives of applicable statutes and which minimize any increase in the cost of credit for small entities."[57] The review panel, which includes individuals from the CFPB, Office of Management and Budget (OMB), and the Small Business Administration's (SBA's) Chief Counsel for Advocacy, must issue a report of the panel's findings as part of the rulemaking process.[58]

Bank regulators are also required by the Small Business Regulatory Enforcement Fairness Act (SBREFA; P.L. 104-121) to develop small entity compliance guides for each final rule that the agency determines has a significant economic impact on a substantial number of small entities.[59] The compliance guides are intended to explain what a small bank must do to comply with the rule. In past years, banking regulators have not consistently fulfilled this requirement. For example, the Office of the Inspector General (OIG) of the Federal Reserve found in July 2013 that the Fed "was not consistent in developing or updating small entity compliance guides in accordance with SBREFA requirements."[60] When the OIG report was published, management at the Fed "concurred with [the] recommendations and stated that it will take steps to implement the recommendations."[61]

In addition to considering a rule's effect on small banks when issuing the rule, regulators also review a rule's impact after it takes effect. Under the Economic Growth and Regulatory Paperwork Reduction Act of 1996 (EGRPRA; P.L. 104-208, 12 U.S.C. §3311), federal banking agencies are required to conduct a review at least every 10 years "to identify outdated or otherwise unnecessary regulatory requirements imposed on insured depository institutions." The act also requires the agencies to seek public comment and submit a report to Congress. The agencies began the latest review process by seeking public comment in June 2014. In this review, the agencies are placing an emphasis on reducing the regulatory burden on community banks.[62]

Agency Interaction and Outreach With Small Banks

Bank regulators have taken a number of steps which they say make them more responsive to the needs of community banks. In the FDIC's statement of policy on rulemaking, it states that "Particular attention is focused on the impact that a regulation will have on small institutions and whether there are comprehensive or targeted alternatives to accomplish the FDIC's goal which would minimize any burden on small institutions. Typically, when notice and opportunity for comment is involved, comment is sought on these matters."[63] Some recent rules have been issued with "Community Bank Guides" to aid community bank compliance.

For recurring or important issues, regulators issue written supervisory guidance to help ensure compliance. At the beginning of supervisory and regulatory letters issued by the Fed, for example, is a statement of applicability that identifies whether the letter is applicable to community banks.[64] According to one Fed official, "This additional clarity not only allows community bankers to focus their efforts on the supervisory policies that are applicable to their banks but it also helps to reduce the chance that examiners will inadvertently subject community banks to large bank expectations."[65]

The Fed has Community Depository Institution Advisory Councils at each of the 12 regional banks, which "regularly collect input from community depository organizations on a number of topics, including ways to reduce regulatory burden and to improve the efficiency of our supervision."[66] The CFPB also has small bank advisory councils. In 2009, the FDIC created a Community Bank Advisory Committee composed of community bank executives to guide it on policy issues that affect small banks and the communities they serve.[67]

The banking regulators have improved outreach to the community banking industry with numerous web resources, seminars, and newsletters. For example, the Fed maintains a Community Banking Connections website that provides "guidance, resources, and tools to help community banks."[68] The FDIC also conducts roundtables, research, and conferences devoted to community banks.[69] The OCC has published research on ways in which community banks can reduce costs.[70]

Supervision and Enforcement

Regulatory burden can also result from supervision and enforcement actions. This section reviews the various ways that regulators have incorporated differential treatment for small banks into the supervision and enforcement processes.

Separate Supervision of Small Banks within and Across Agencies

Small and large banks are supervised in different ways, with one of the differences being who does the supervision and how. As mentioned above in the "Who Regulates Banks and What Do Regulators Do?" section, banks are examined for safety and soundness and for consumer protection. Large banks have their supervision divided between prudential regulators for safety and soundness and the CFPB for consumer protection, but the two supervisory responsibilities are combined for banks with $10 billion or less in assets. Some consider it less burdensome to interact with one regulator rather than two, although small banks are still examined separately by the primary regulator for safety and soundness and consumer protection. Likewise, different subsidiaries of the same institution may be regulated by different regulators.

Banks are assigned a prudential regulator based on their charter. Different regulators supervising banks in different ways could lead to disparate levels of regulatory burden. To ensure consistency and to harmonize supervision *across* regulators, the banking regulators coordinate through the Federal Financial Institutions Examination Council (FFIEC). The FFIEC offers bank examiner training programs and has developed a uniform bank rating system that is employed by the prudential regulators. These and other efforts are intended to promote consistency across bank regulators.

Regulatory burden issues occur not just across regulators, but *within* bank regulators. Regulators supervise banks of different sizes. Some are concerned that supervision practices that are intended to apply only to large banks could trickle down to small banks.[71]

One way that regulators address these issues is by structuring their internal organization so that different parts of the agency have responsibility for supervising different banks:

- The OCC has a senior deputy comptroller for Midsize/Community Banking Supervision and a senior deputy comptroller for Large Bank Supervision. The OCC also has separate booklets in the *Comptroller's Handbook* that describe the different ways that large banks and community banks are to be examined.[72]
- A subcommittee of Fed Board members on Smaller Regional and Community Banking was established in 2011 "with a primary goal ... [of] an understanding of the unique characteristics of community and regional banks and ... the potential for excessive burden and adverse effects on lending. Since its establishment, the subcommittee has led a number of initiatives focused on reducing regulatory burden on community banking organizations ... "[73] The Fed has a separate supervisory framework for banks with $50 billion or more in assets, banks with between $10 billion and $50 billion, and banks with less than $10 billion in assets "to take account of differences in business models, risks, relative regulatory burden, and other salient considerations."[74]
- The FDIC has a separate Office of Complex Financial Institutions that focuses on large and complex financial institutions; the Division of Risk Management Supervision examines the remaining FDIC-supervised institutions. To give additional emphasis to community banks, each FDIC examiner is "initially trained as a community bank examiner" before potentially specializing in other areas.[75]

Examinations

On-site examinations, also referred to as visitorial powers, are part of the supervisory process. A regulator's visitorial powers include

> (i) Examination of a bank; (ii) Inspection of a bank's books and records; (iii) Regulation and supervision of activities authorized or permitted pursuant to federal banking law; and (iv) Enforcing compliance with any applicable Federal or state laws concerning those activities, including through investigations that seek to ascertain compliance through production of non-public information by the bank... [with certain limitations].[76]

Regulators examine banks at least once every 12 months, but banks with less than $500 million in total assets that have high supervisory ratings and meet certain conditions are examined once every 18 months.[77] Regulators changed the frequency of examinations in 2007 from once every 12 months to once every 18 months pursuant to the Financial Services Regulatory Relief Act (P.L. 109-351).[78] In contrast, some large and complex banks have examiners conducting full-time monitoring on-site. The bank receives a report of the findings when an examination is completed.

Bank regulators have established multiple processes for a bank to appeal the results of its examination. Regulators typically encourage a bank to attempt to resolve any dispute informally through discussions with the bank examiner.[79] The Riegle Community Development and Regulatory Improvement Act of 1994 required banking regulators to establish a formal appeals process for supervisory findings, appoint an independent ombudsman, and create safeguards to prevent retaliation against a bank that disputes their examination findings.[80]

Regulators have taken steps to reduce the regulatory burden associated with on-site examinations. The Fed introduced a new examination program in January 2014 that, according to Governor Tarullo, "more explicitly links examination intensity to the individual community bank's risk profile.... The new program calls for examiners to spend less time on low-risk compliance issues at community banks."[81] In testimony before the Senate Banking Committee, Governor Tarullo also stated, "Recognizing the burden that the on-site presence of many examiners can place on the day-to-day business of a community bank, we are also working to increase our level of off-site supervisory activities.... To that end, last year we completed a pilot on conducting parts of the labor-intensive loan review off-site using electronic records from banks."[82]

Reporting and Data Collection

Bank supervision is not a one-time event that occurs when the examiner visits the bank, but rather is an ongoing process that includes monitoring data collected from banks. The number of reports that a bank must submit depends on its size and activities. The primary source of data is the quarterly Reports of Condition and Income, or call report, that the bank submits to its regulator.

The FDIC has argued that call reports "provide an early indication that an institution's risk profile may be changing" and are therefore important parts of the supervision process.[83] The call report is structured to lower the burden on small banks relative to larger and more complex banks. The FDIC states that the

> Call Report itself is tiered to size and complexity of the filing institution, in that more than one-third of the data items are linked to asset size or activity levels. Based on this tiering alone, community banks never, or rarely, need to fill out a number of pages in the Call Report, not counting the data items and pages that are not applicable to a particular bank based on its business model. For example, a typical $75 million community bank showed reportable amounts in only 14 percent of the data items in the Call Report and provided data on 40 pages. Even a relatively large community bank, at $1.3 billion, showed reportable amounts in only 21 percent of data items and provided data on 47 pages.[84]

Bank regulators have also taken other steps to reduce the burden associated with regulatory reporting. Just as banks file call reports, small bank and thrift holding companies must submit the Consolidated Financial Statements for Bank Holding Companies (the FR Y-9 series). The Fed, which oversees holding companies, recently announced that the reporting requirements for the FR Y-9 series will be reduced for those holding companies with less than $1 billion in total assets that meet certain criteria.[85]

Even though the CFPB is not the primary supervisor for consumer protection of small banks, the CFPB and the prudential bank regulators are required to collaborate on data requests and examinations as a means of reducing regulatory burden. As described in CRS Report, *The Consumer Financial Protection Bureau (CFPB): A Legal Analysis*, by David H. Carpenter,

> prudential regulators must provide the CFPB access to all reports, records, and other documents connected to the examination; must allow

the CFPB examiners to participate in all aspects of the examination; and generally must take into account any input that the CFPB's examiner offers regarding the examination. Also, the Bureau may require reports directly from these depositories, although the Bureau will have to rely on existing reports "to the fullest extent possible."

Enforcement

When an issue is identified during the supervisory process, bank regulators may require a bank to take corrective measures. As with the appeals process for examinations, there are informal and formal approaches. During the examination process, bank examiners may ask the bank to voluntarily agree to take a corrective action to ensure that it complies with a law or regulation. In some cases, regulators take a more formal approach to compel the bank to take a required action, such as through a prompt corrective action directive or cease and desist order, and may impose monetary and other penalties on the bank. Banks may devote resources to legal expertise to understand enforcement actions that apply to others, thus adding to their own regulatory burden. Frequently, banks and regulators reach settlements to avoid legal actions. Some banks have complained that settlements against their competitors can result in additional regulatory burden upon them, because the terms of the settlement become the new industry standard.

Enforcement actions taken against other banks may discourage a bank from performing certain business functions that they may in fact be allowed to perform. Generally, to provide transparency, regulators publicly disclose formal enforcement actions on their website.

Summary of Treatment of Small Banks in Rulemaking, Supervision, and Enforcement

Regulatory burden can be manifested in multiple ways in each stage of the regulatory process— rulemaking, supervision, and enforcement. Small banks are exempt from many rules, especially recent ones, and the regulations that do apply to small banks are often tailored to reduce their regulatory burden. In addition, financial regulators are required to give consideration during the rulemaking process about what effect rules would have on small banks. Supervision and enforcement are also structured to pose less of a burden on small banks than larger banks.

Because of this requisite differential treatment of small and large banks, one could argue that there not is a "one-size-fits-all" approach to bank regulation. Most aspects of the regulation of small banks are designed to impose less of a burden on small banks than larger banks, but that does not necessarily prove whether the existing regulatory structure is unduly burdensome for small banks. Thus, if small banks are facing unduly burdensome regulation, it is either in absolute terms, as a result of numerous rulemakings implementing the Dodd-Frank Act and other recent acts, or because small banks have less capacity for regulatory compliance than large banks (because there is economies to scale to regulatory compliance, for example), and not because small banks face relatively more regulatory burden than large banks. Even though aspects of regulation are different for small and large banks, it is possible that the exemptions and tailoring for small banks may be inefficiently targeted, and small banks might be able to benefit from additional regulatory relief without undermining the goals of protecting consumers, enhancing the safety and soundness of banks, and promoting financial stability.

RATIONALES OFFERED FOR REGULATING SMALL AND LARGE BANKS DIFFERENTLY

As discussed in the last section, a safety and soundness focus on minimizing risk to the taxpayer, which was perceived to be independent of size, favored a unitary model of bank regulation. Governor Tarullo highlighted the role of systemic risk in the crisis as a rationale for moving away from the unitary model, described in more detail next. Other possible rationales for moving away from the unitary model follow.

Systemic Risk

Since the recent financial crisis, regulatory emphasis has been placed on mitigating systemic risk—risks posed to financial stability. There are numerous potential sources of systemic risk, including activities undertaken by small banks. Indeed, systemic risk concerns related to bank runs underlie the economic rationale for the creation of the Fed and deposit insurance. Nevertheless, given the role of large banks in the crisis, policymakers have been particularly focused on the systemic risk posed by large banks and ensuring that they are not "too big to fail" (meaning that policymakers would "bail them out" to prevent their failure because of systemic risk concerns).[86] The Dodd-Frank Act attempted to address this problem by imposing heightened prudential regulatory standards on the largest banks relative to small and medium-sized banks.

There are several rationales for this approach. First, if a large bank and its creditors believed that policymakers would intervene to prevent its failure, it would face moral hazard, meaning there would be less incentive to monitor the firm's riskiness. Heightened regulation could safeguard against the tendency for the firm to increase its riskiness in light of moral hazard. Second, heightened regulation would be a way to potentially help "level the playing field" if too big to fail provides large banks with a funding advantage over smaller banks (because the likelihood of a bailout in case of failure is priced into its funding costs.) Third, if the failure of a large firm poses systemic risk and the failure of a small firm does not, then policymakers would want to make it less likely that large firms would fail than small firms. Similarly, if it is less likely that policymakers will impose losses on creditors of large failed banks on systemic risk grounds, then it is more likely that losses will be imposed on taxpayers in the event of a failure. Thus, heightened regulation could make it less likely that large banks will fail and impose losses on taxpayers. Critics of the enhanced prudential regime believe that regulatory capture could exacerbate the moral hazard problem without effectively curbing risk taking.

A common variation on this theme is the argument that small banks did not *cause* the crisis, and therefore should not be *punished* with new regulations. Although it is beyond the scope of this report to determine to what extent small or large banks caused the crisis, hundreds of small banks failed during the financial crisis,[87] depleting the FDIC's deposit insurance fund and placing taxpayers at risk. A case can be made that small banks do not need to face regulatory safeguards that are as stringent as large banks because they pose less systemic risk. But systemic risk is only one of the goals of regulation, and a case can also be made that pre-crisis regulations for small banks were not stringent enough to protect the deposit insurance fund. In other words, if there are macroprudential reasons for having relatively less stringent safety and soundness regulation on small banks than large banks, there are also microprudential arguments for having more stringent regulation in absolute terms on small banks than was in place before the crisis.

Economies of Scale to Compliance

Another potential rationale for regulating small banks differently from large banks would be if there are economies of scale to regulatory compliance costs. The costs of compliance include investment in software and information systems, manpower, and specialized knowledge (legal expertise, accounting expertise, and so on). In absolute terms, regulatory compliance costs are likely to rise with size, but regulatory compliance might involve fewer resources for large firms than small firms proportional to overall revenues. In particular, as regulatory complexity increases, compliance may become relatively more costly for small firms than large firms.

From a cost-benefit perspective, if regulatory compliance costs are subject to economies of scale, then the balance of costs and benefits of a particular regulation will differ depending on the size of the bank. For the same regulatory proposal, economies of scale could potentially result in costs outweighing benefits for smaller banks but the benefits outweighing costs for larger banks. In these instances, exemptions or simplified regulations could be warranted for small banks on cost-benefit grounds. In other cases, the benefits might be large enough to outweigh costs to small banks even in the presence of economies of scale.

Empirical evidence on whether compliance costs are subject to economies of scale is hampered by the FDIC's finding that banks are unable to disentangle regulatory compliance costs from general operating costs.[88] A study by the FDIC's inspector general provides some evidence of economies of scale in compliance. It found that exams of banks with less than $50 million in assets averaged 335 hours, whereas banks with $500 million-$1 billion in assets averaged 850 hours in 2011. In other words, exams for larger banks took longer, but the increase in hours was not linear with the increase in assets.[89] A 2013 CFPB study on the costs associated with certain regulations found some evidence of economies of scale to compliance, but noted that because it used a case study model that focused on just seven banks, it did not draw broad generalizations from its findings.[90] A survey[91] of members by the Independent Community Banks Association showed mixed evidence of economies of scale in call report compliance. For banks with less than $500 million in assets, costs were similar regardless of the banks' size, but for banks with more than $500 million in assets, costs were significantly higher than for banks with less than $500 million in assets. Because the survey was of members and members are generally small, it did not contain evidence for call report compliance costs for the largest banks, however.

Critical Mass

Another potential reason for exempting small banks from (or tailoring) certain regulations would be if few banks within a class (based on size or some other metric) engage in that activity. In other words, banks within a class would be subject to the regulation only if there were a critical mass of banks for which it was relevant.[92]

For any given area of regulation, there might not be a critical mass among small banks because of differences in business model from large banks. Or there could be no critical mass because regulation is aimed at policy issues that are perceived to exist primarily at large banks. For example, Tarullo recently highlighted the Volcker Rule (i.e., the prohibition on proprietary trading and sponsoring hedge funds) as a rule applying to all banks, but which he argued that the activities of small banks were unlikely to pose the problems that the Volcker Rule was intended to address.[93]

This issue could also be considered from a cost-benefit perspective—while regulators might forgo some benefits by exempting those institutions from within a class that are active in the area of concern, those benefits might not outweigh the costs that would be imposed on the nonactive institutions within the class. For example, the regulation of activities might have nontrivial compliance costs for nonparticipants (e.g., the costs of demonstrating to regulators that a bank is complying with rules in an area where that bank is not active). Moreover, if few in the class have a risk exposure in a given area, there is less likelihood that that risk would pose systemic concerns. Applying exemptions on the grounds of lack of critical mass would arguably be best done on a case-by case basis. Within a cost-benefit framework, there would still likely be cases where the benefits of regulating a few small banks that participated in an activity outweighed the costs of regulating the rest that did not.

Creating Advantages for Small Banks

Some policymakers would like to tailor regulation to favor small banks because they believe small banks provide a unique public benefit. Generally, some argue for reducing the regulatory burden on small banks on the grounds that they provide greater access to credit or offer credit at lower prices than large banks. (Empirical evidence on this is mixed—for example, data indicate that small banks make relatively fewer residential mortgages and credit card loans than large banks but make relatively more small business loans.)[94] Theoretically, market forces should ensure that the lowest price and highest supply of credit that the market will bear will prevail if markets are perfectly competitive; if small banks are offering broader access to credit or lower prices, they will succeed in drawing business without preferential policy. In this framework, creating differences in regulatory burden based on size would distort the efficient allocation of credit. If markets are not perfectly competitive (because large banks might have some market power, for example) or the regulatory burden already differs by size, then those results might not hold. For example, the costs of regulatory compliance (notably, the large amount of capital required to start a bank) may impose a barrier to entry that favors incumbents and reduces competition.

Arguments about the importance of small banks tend to emphasize niches they fill where, it is claimed, larger banks would be ill equipped to replace them, such as in rural and underserved areas. Data to support these arguments include the fact that community banks held 71% of total deposits in rural counties in 2011 (compared with 19% of overall deposits).[95] Some argue that rules must be more flexible or include exemptions for small banks to be able to extend adequate credit to rural and underserved areas. Examples of this principle can be found in existing regulation—for example, lenders in rural areas have additional compliance options for the Ability-to-Repay rule that are not available to some other banks.[96] Similarly, it is argued that small banks are better situated to engage in types of transactions that depend on "relationship banking" (i.e., personalized knowledge of risks). For example, data indicate that small banks make relatively more agricultural loans than large banks.[97] It is argued that rigid regulations with standardized criteria are not well suited for the relationship banking model.[98] Alternatively, if the policy goal is to help rural or underserved communities, it could arguably be more efficient to target those populations directly, rather than providing regulatory relief to small banks regardless of how much credit they provide to those populations.

Some may want to protect community banks out of a preference for their traditional business model. Community banks are also more likely to engage in portfolio lending, as opposed to the originate-to-distribute (securitization) model; some policymakers prefer the former, given the role the latter played in the crisis.[99]

Ultimately, evaluating arguments about the desirability of reducing their regulatory burden in order to promote small banks requires subjective value judgments about the relative desirability of competing policy goals. While some want to reduce the burden on small banks for the reasons cited above, others argue that reducing the burden on banks by exempting them from certain rules could lead to regulatory arbitrage—moving activities to less regulated entities in order to avoid regulation. Regulatory arbitrage could result in disparate treatment for consumers, for example, as consumers might only have protections when they operate at some institutions but not at others.

Empirical Evidence of the Regulatory Burden on Small Banks

This report has explained how small and large banks are regulated and how that regulation can translate into regulatory burden. Quantifying the magnitude of regulatory burden for banks has been a challenge for researchers, including the FDIC, GAO, and CFPB.[100] The FDIC's "Community Banking Study" found,

> In an attempt to quantify the cost of regulatory compliance at their institution, interview participants were asked whether they tracked regulatory compliance costs within their internal cost structure. All the interview participants indicated that they did not actively track the various costs associated with regulatory compliance, because it is too time-consuming, costly, and is so interwoven into their operations that it would be difficult to break out these specific costs.[101]

In September 2012, GAO reported to Congress that "[i]ndustry officials told us that it is difficult to know for sure which provisions [of the Dodd-Frank Act] will impact community banks and credit unions, because the outcome largely depends on how agencies implement certain provisions through their rules, and many of the rules implementing the act have not been finalized."[102] Since then, GAO has issued other reports on the Dodd-Frank Act rulemaking but has not attempted to quantify the regulatory burden on small banks.

A November 2013 CFPB case study of the regulatory burden in the area of consumer protection looked at compliance costs at seven banks of varying size for four regulations. It found that compliance costs for certain regulations as a percentage of retail operating expense at the two banks in the study with less than $1 billion in assets were 3.9% and 5.6% of retail deposit operating expense, respectively—more than double the percentage for the banks with more than $1 billion in assets.[103] It costs the smaller banks relatively more to comply than the larger banks. As the CFPB notes, "Seven case studies do not, however, justify broad generalizations— especially about scale effects..."[104] The CFPB report also describes the challenges it faced in analyzing regulatory burden, including that banks "generally do not track their full costs of compliance, and the relevant information is often scattered across several departments and many employees."[105]

One reason that only incomplete information on regulatory burden exists is because no statute requires regulators to make quantitative estimates for all rules that they issue. As discussed in the "Special Consideration in Statute for Small Banks in the Rulemaking Process" section above, there are three types of statutory requirements that provide some information on regulatory burden:

- Pursuant to 12 U.S.C. §4802, banking regulators are generally required to "consider costs" and benefits but do not necessarily have to perform a quantitative cost-benefit analysis. **Table 3** summarizes how bank regulators reported costs and benefits for the 14 major rules pursuant to the Dodd-Frank Act. It shows that regulators did not quantify overall costs or benefits for any of these rules. The prudential regulators quantified some costs (while qualitatively discussing benefits) for two rules, qualitatively discussed costs and benefits for three rules, and CRS could not locate any cost-benefit analysis for the other four rules. The CFPB quantified some costs (while qualitatively discussing benefits) for two rules and qualitatively discussed costs and benefits for three rules.[106] Generally speaking, costs and benefits for small banks might be qualitatively discussed in these analyses, but quantitative estimates did not break out effects on small banks.
- The Regulatory Flexibility Act requires regulators to perform an assessment only for rules that are determined to have a significant economic impact on a substantial number of small entities. In their RFA analysis, the regulators use a lower threshold for small entities (currently, $500 million or less in assets) than the definition of small bank used by the FDIC, Fed, or OCC. **Table 3** summarizes whether the regulators found a significant economic impact on a substantial number of small entities for the 14 major rules pursuant to the Dodd-Frank Act. The prudential regulators found no significant impact on small entities for seven rules and could not determine whether there was a significant impact for one rule. They found that one rule, the Basel III Regulatory Capital rule, may have a significant impact, estimating that 146 banks with less than $500 million in assets (out of 5,638 overall) faced a capital shortfall of $620 million, certain

compliance costs of $43,000 per institution, and lost tax benefits totaling $3.4 million per year under the rule when fully phased in.[107] The CFPB could not rule out that any of the five rules it issued would not have a significant impact on small entities. In one case, it did not know how many small entities would be affected, and in four other cases, it estimated that more than 3,700 banks or thrifts (as well as credit unions and non-banks) with less than $175 million in assets participated in the activity addressed by the rule, although it provided no quantitative estimate of the costs to those firms or how many would be covered by the exemptions or tailoring provided in the rules.

- The Paperwork Reduction Act (P.L. 104-13) requires regulators to estimate the hours that banks spend complying with its requests for information. Agencies must report this information to the OMB's Office of Information and Regulatory Affairs (OIRA), which posts it on its website.[108] Although the hours spent complying with regulators' requests for information is just one component of regulatory burden, agencies do not break the data out to distinguish between hours spent by small and large banks, further complicating the effort to estimate the magnitude of regulatory burden for small banks.

Table 3. Summary of Cost-Benefit and Regulatory Flexibility Act Analyses for Recent "Major Rules" Issued by Bank Regulators Pursuant to the Dodd-Frank Act

Official Title	RIN	C-B Analysis Performed?	Was There a "Significant Economic Impact on Small Entities"?
Liquidity Coverage Ratio: Liquidity Risk Measurement Standards	1557-AD74	Prudential Regulators OCC quantified costs, provided qualitative benefits (FDIC and Fed did not perform)	no
Regulatory Capital Rules: Regulatory Capital, Revisions to the Supplementary Leverage Ratio	1557-AD74	OCC quantified costs, provided qualitative benefits (FDIC and Fed did not perform)	no

Official Title	RIN	C-B Analysis Performed?	Was There a "Significant Economic Impact on Small Entities"?
Prohibitions and Restrictions on Proprietary Trading and Certain Interests in, and Relationships With, Hedge Funds and Private Equity Funds ("Volcker Rule")	7100-AD82	none	no
Treatment Of Certain Collateralized Debt Obligations Backed Primarily By Trust Preferred Securities With Regard To Prohibitions And Restrictions On Certain Interests In, And Relationships With, Hedge Funds And Private Equity Funds	1557-AD79	none	no
Regulatory Capital Rules: Regulatory Capital, Implementation Of Basel III, Capital Adequacy, Transition Provisions, Prompt Corrective Action, Standardized Approach For Risk-Weighted Assets, Market Discipline And Disclosure Requirements, Advanced Approaches Risk-Based Capital Rule, And Market Risk Capital Rule	1557-AD46, 3064-AD95a	qualitative discussion by agencies; quantitative global study of costs and benefits by Financial Stability Board before the U.S. rule was proposed	maybe; 146 banks with less than $500 million in assets (out of 5,638 overall) faced a capital shortfall of $620 million, lost tax benefits totaling $3.4 million per year, and certain compliance costs of $43,000 per institution under the rule when fully phased in
Risk-Based Capital Guidelines: Market Risk	1557-AC99	qualitative discussion	no
Debit Card Interchange Fees And Routing	7100-AD63	qualitative discussion (Fed concluded it does not know if costs outweigh benefits)	despite exemption, do not know

Table 3. (Continued)

Official Title	RIN	C-B Analysis Performed?	Was There a "Significant Economic Impact on Small Entities"?
Enhanced Prudential Standards For Bank Holding Companies And Foreign Banking Organizations	7100-AD86	none	no
Supervision And Regulation Assessments For Bank Holding Companies And Savings And Loan Holding Companies With Total Consolidated Assets Of $50 Billion Or More And Nonbank Financial Companies Supervised By The Federal Reserve	7100-AD95	none	no
	Consumer Financial Protection Bureau		
Ability-To-Repay And Qualified Mortgage Standards Under The Truth In Lending Act (Regulation Z)	3170-AA17	some costs quantified, other costs and benefits discussed qualitatively	cannot rule it out, rule affects 3,839 banks and thrifts with <$175m in assets; no estimate of costs
Electronic Fund Transfers (Regulation E)	3170-AA15	qualitative discussion of costs and benefits	cannot rule it out, do not know how many or cost
Loan Originator Compensation Requirements Under the Truth In Lending Act (Regulation Z)	3170-AA13	qualitative discussion of costs and benefits	cannot rule it out, rule affects 3,839 small banks and thrifts with <$175m in assets; no estimate of costs
Mortgage Servicing Rules Under the Real Estate Settlement Procedures Act (Regulation X)	3170-AA14	qualitative discussion of costs and benefits	cannot rule it out, rule affects 3,714 small banks and thrifts with <$175m in assets; no cost estimate

Official Title	RIN	C-B Analysis Performed?	Was There a "Significant Economic Impact on Small Entities"?
Mortgage Servicing Rules Under the Truth In Lending Act (Regulation Z)	3170-AA14	some costs quantified, other costs and benefits discussed qualitatively	cannot rule it out, rule affects 3,714 small banks and thrifts with <$175m in assets; no estimate of costs

Source: CRS analysis of rules and supporting documents, GAO reports under the Congressional Review Act Note: RIN = "Regulation Identifier Number."

[a] CRS has combined two rules issued separately by regulators on separate dates that are substantively the same.

In summary, all three of these requirements result in the regulators estimating only partial—if any—costs associated with regulation. Estimates are made before rules are implemented and are generally not revisited after the fact to test their accuracy. In any case, all of these statutory requirements apply only to the issuance of new rules, which are just one subset of the sources of overall regulatory burden; there are no statutory requirements for regulators to estimates the costs associated with regulation (rulemaking, supervision, and enforcement) as a whole. Because estimates are typically made for individual rules in isolation, there is little understanding of what happens to overall burden when rules are aggregated.

Although quantitative assessments may help policymakers understand the magnitude of the regulatory burden associated with new and existing regulations, there are reasonable arguments for why they should not be performed. In their qualitative assessments, regulators often detail the multiple unknowns that would make a quantitative estimate subject to considerable uncertainty. Regulators issue hundreds of new rules annually, some of which involve relatively minor changes; quantitative requirements could significantly increase the resources required for rulemaking or potentially slow down the rulemaking process. Regulators have noted the difficulty of performing accurate cost-benefit assessments for some complex rules. For example, a Fed official testified,

> the challenges (sic) is that it's easy to measure the cost because they fall to specific institutions. It's much harder to measure the benefits because they really accrue to a very broad population. Things like safety and soundness of the banking system or confidence in the payment

system. Analyses that include a high degree of uncertainty could potentially be misleading and do more harm than good.[109]

Furthermore, the requests for data and the additional information that could be necessary to perform more detailed studies could themselves result in more regulatory burden.

Regulators do not regularly report data on the burden stemming from supervision. Sometimes they produce one-time studies, however. In response to a congressional request, bank regulators' inspectors general conducted studies on the regulatory burden to small banks stemming from compliance with supervisory exams. From 2007 to 2011, OCC community bank exams typically took 120 days or less (as they are intended to), but sometimes took up to a year, and occasionally took over a year.[110] The length of exams was slightly longer from 2008 to 2010, when the most banks were failing. In 2011, FDIC community bank risk-management exams varied in length from an average of 335 hours to 1,820 hours based on the size of the bank and its supervisory rating. From 2007 to 2011, exams of banks with poor supervisory ratings became shorter over time and banks with good supervisory ratings took longer over time. In addition, the FDIC conducts thousands of compliance and a few CRA exams annually. In 2011, the FDIC spent an average of 24 days to 57 days on-site for risk management exams, based on supervisory rating.[111] Fed exams (not including state-led exams, which took longer), averaged 63 days to 79 days between 2007 and 2011, peaking in 2009.[112] Although costs cannot be derived directly from hours spent on exams, this data may nevertheless give some indication of regulatory burden caused by meeting with examination staff and uncertainty created while waiting for exam results.

By statute (12 U.S.C. §4806), banks may appeal exam results to the agency Ombudsman. The frequency of appeals might give some indication of bank displeasure with the examination process. The IGs report that banks only formally appealed 22 OCC exam results (informally appealed 24 more), 23 FDIC exams (informally appealed 18 more), and 12 Fed exams (no informal appeal data) out of the thousands of exams performed between 2007 and 2011. However, banks might not appeal an exam result they thought was unfair if they thought their appeal had no chance of succeeding. As noted above, many disputes are resolved through the supervisory process, before an exam is completed.

There is no official data on the regulatory burden associated with call reports. The Independent Community Bankers of America (ICBA), a trade association representing community banks, conducted a survey, however, which found that "[a]lmost three quarters of respondents stated that the number of hours required to complete the call report had increased over the last ten years. Over one third of respondents indicated a significant increase in hours over this period. Well over three quarters of respondents noted increased costs in call report preparation with almost one third noting that costs increased significantly."[113] As noted above, regulators argue that the call reports are already tailored to reduce the burden on small banks.

Studies have attempted to estimate the regulatory burden of specific policies,[114] but there is a dearth of empirical evidence on the overall regulatory burden posed by bank regulation. Because there are no official quantitative estimates of—or data sources for—the absolute regulatory burden on the banking system as a whole, it is impossible to provide empirical evidence that gives an overall answer to the two the questions pertinent to this report: (1) what is the absolute regulatory burden on small banks and how has it changed? and (2) what is the burden on small banks relative to large banks and how has it changed?

OPTIONS TO ACCOUNT FOR SIZE IN ALTERNATIVE REGULATORY MODELS

If Governor Tarullo is correct that recent rulemaking has resulted in a *de facto* shift away from the unitary model, Congress may choose to consider what model would best achieve its policy priorities. Rather than discuss the many provisions of bank regulation or supervisory practices that could be modified to provide regulatory relief within the existing system, this section focuses on the different ways that the regulatory system could be structured to account for size, presenting the pros and cons of each approach. The spectrum of options ranges from regulating banks in the same way regardless of size to a separate regulatory regime for small banks and large banks, with various approaches in between.

Maintain Status Quo (Ad Hoc Exemptions)

Absent change to the status quo, all banks will continue to be assigned a primary regulator by charter and subject to the same regulations except in cases where exemptions or tailoring based on size has been provided by statute or regulator discretion. In addition, some current exemptions that are not based on size might still tend to disproportionately benefit small banks, such as exemptions for banks operating in rural or underserved areas. As new laws and regulations are adopted, policymakers will decide on a case-by-case basis whether the law or rulemaking will have a size-based exemption or tailoring, and if so, what size threshold to use. New legislation can also be used to retroactively add or amend size exemptions in existing statute.[115]

The advantage of this ad hoc approach is that exemptions can theoretically be individually tailored to the optimum size for each policy issue, given that the optimal size is likely to vary by issue based on the regulation's purpose. The disadvantage is a lack of coherence and consistency in the overall regulatory structure, which is likely to add to the overall complexity and burden of regulation. Some might argue that ad hoc exemption levels are not set at optimal levels based on some objective standard in practice, but are instead arbitrarily chosen based on fluid political dynamics. Maintaining the status quo model might also make it more difficult to address existing regulations where policymakers believe an exemption should be added, since regulations would have to be altered individually, and there is no mechanism in place to revisit them expeditiously.

Institute Consistent Exemption Size

A variation on the status quo would be to move to a consistent exemption size for all regulations with exemptions set by statute or the regulators. Such a system could give regulators discretion as when to apply exemptions or include standardized criteria in statute for when exemptions should be applied.[116] The advantages and disadvantages of this option—more consistency and predictability, less flexibility—would be the inverse of the advantages and disadvantages discussed in the status quo section. Whether it reduced the regulatory burden on small banks compared to the status quo would depend on where the exemption was set and how frequently regulators applied it. Were policymakers to adopt a standard exemption, they could also consider whether there should be a process for retroactively applying it to existing regulations.

Were policymakers to move to a single exemption level, the question would be whether the exemption should be set relatively high, so that regulations with exemptions only applied to very large, complex banks, who tend to be active internationally and have non-bank subsidiaries with substantial operations, or whether exemptions should be set relatively low, so that it applied only to relatively small banks that tended to have simple business models.[117] In other words, the question would be how many – if any – of the banks in the middle of the spectrum (often referred to in policy debates as "regional banks") should be exempt.

A variation on a standard exemption level would be to have regulators set varying exemption levels based on some standard criteria or standardized process that has been formulated ex ante. For example, regulators could be required to set the exemption threshold so that the benefits of the regulation outweighed the costs. This could result in more appropriately tailored exemption levels than a standard exemption, but would entail more time and resources on the part of regulators. It would arguably not result in a simpler regulatory system than the status quo.

A unitary model with a consistent exemption size would not address concerns for and against the next two options regarding regulatory specialization or a level playing field.

A System with Size-Based Charters

As discussed above, different bank charters exist in statute, but differences in operations and regulations between charters have blurred over time. Eligibility for charters is not based on size; although thrifts and credit unions are smaller than banks on average, there are also large thrifts and credit unions. One policy option would be to replace the current system with charters and regulators based on a size threshold. For example, there could be a "community bank" charter and a "large complex organization" charter, and a separate regulator to administer each charter. Modifying the basis of charters might naturally lend itself to a broader reevaluation of the optimum number of charters and regulators—a reduction in which could in itself be conducive to reducing regulatory burden and complexity.

The potential advantage of this system would be that regulations could be more attuned to differences in large and small banks' business models. Regulators often tailor regulations now, but a separate charter would be the simplest way to guarantee it. With a division of labor, each regulator could be more specialized, knowledgeable, and sensitive to the unique issues facing the banks that it regulated. Taken to the extreme, two fundamentally separate and distinct regulatory architectures could emerge, as has happened with credit unions and banks. This might allow for simpler and less burdensome regulation for small banks (depending on how their regulator behaved), but two systems would arguably be more complex overall than one.

The potential advantage of this system could turn out to be a weakness, however, because it could make the system more susceptible to “regulatory capture,” even if Congress chose to put safeguards in place to prevent it. Regulatory capture is the concept that regulators work in the interests of the entities that they regulate instead of the public interest. A size-based charter could make it more likely that the small bank regulator worked in the interests of the small banks and the large bank regulator worked in the interest of the large banks. It would also follow that it could be more likely that the regulators and the regulations that they issued would be in conflict with one another, perhaps creating opportunities for regulatory arbitrage.

Some might see parallels between such a proposal and perceived regulatory capture problems with the former Office of Thrift Supervision (OTS). OTS regulated thrifts, which began as mostly small institutions with a statutorily limited business model. Over time, regulatory differences between banks and thrifts eroded, and it was claimed that some firms chose a thrift charter (called charter shopping) because OTS was the least onerous federal regulator.[118] The Dodd-Frank Act abolished the OTS (but kept the thrift charter) out of the widely held belief that the OTS had been captured by thrifts and was insufficiently monitoring their riskiness.[119] In contrast, it might be argued that problems with OTS were not relevant to a size-based charter. One problem with the OTS was that it was believed to lack the expertise or perhaps the authority to adequately regulate a few very large, complex organizations, such as Washington Mutual, AIG, and Lehman Brothers, that in some cases had very limited depository activities. Basing the charter on a size threshold might avoid problems such as charter shopping and lack of regulatory expertise, if the threshold was applied at the holding company level rather than the depository subsidiary level.

“Level Playing Field” (Unitary Model)

The opposite end of the spectrum from separate chartering would be a “level playing field” or a “true unitary” approach in which regulations were not tailored to account for size or other differences between banks. Moving to a true unitary approach might naturally lend itself to reducing the number of charters and regulators, which could in itself be conducive to reducing regulatory burden and complexity. The advantage of this approach would be to minimize opportunities for regulatory arbitrage—the possibility of activities migrating to banks where the activities are exempt from regulation. This could increase the overall efficiency of financial intermediation and credit allocation. The disadvantages of this approach would be that regulations would be less targeted although banks are diverse, so that some regulations could impose regulatory costs on banks that are not relevant to them.

In cases where small banks were losing exemptions from regulations, it would make them worse off. But in some cases, a level playing field could make small banks better off. For example, some critics of Dodd-Frank's enhanced prudential regulatory regime claim that it is beneficial to large banks because of regulatory capture and that it formalizes their too big to fail status. If this were true, ending the enhanced prudential regulatory regime for large banks would level the playing field to the benefit of small banks.

Whether such an approach resulted in more or less regulatory burden for small banks depends on how current policies with size-based exemptions were reworked. A level playing field approach might be supported whether one is in favor of more or less regulation for banks overall. Whether the focus is on reducing regulatory burden or mitigating risk through enhanced regulation, a case could be made that either goal is better achieved and more likely to succeed if implemented consistently for all banks, regardless of size.

OBSERVATIONS

This report analyzed the relative burden of small versus large banks and finds that small banks have received accommodations in recent major rules and through various supervisory arrangements and outreach. Regulatory burden has increased for small banks in absolute terms since the recent financial crisis, but arguably not in relative terms compared with larger banks. For example, 13 of the 14 "major" rules issued by banking regulators pursuant to the Dodd-Frank Act either include an exemption for small banks or are tailored to reduce the cost for small banks to comply. The remaining rule provided regulatory relief for securities backed by a type of capital frequently issued by small banks.

Recent increases in regulatory burden on an absolute but not relative basis may affect the ability of small banks to compete with non-banks, but should not negatively affect their ability to compete with large banks.[120] This report did not analyze whether the absolute burden is too great because that depends on policymakers' judgments about balancing financial stability, credit availability, consumer protection, and other objectives.

An important distinction drawn by this report is between the concept of *regulatory burden* and the phrase *unduly burdensome*. Whereas regulatory burden is about the costs associated with a regulation, unduly burdensome refers to the balance between the benefits and costs of a regulation. For example, some would consider a regulation to be unduly burdensome if costs are in excess of benefits or if the same benefits could be achieved at a lower cost. But the mere presence of regulatory burden does not mean that a regulation is unduly burdensome.

Overestimating regulatory burden can lead to policies that would repeal or change regulations that may have positive net benefits for consumers, banks, and the broader economy. Underestimating regulatory burden, however, could result in further consolidation in the banking industry, the migration of activity outside the banking system to the shadow banking system, and reduced access and higher cost of credit for rural and underserved areas and small businesses that are customers of small banks. Accurately assessing regulatory burden and determining whether the burden rises to the level of being unduly burdensome, therefore, is important for policymakers to make informed judgments. Quantifying the magnitude of regulatory burden has been a challenge for researchers, however, because banks do not track their compliance costs and regulators do not typically provide estimates of the costs of new rules.

Much of the discussion about unduly burdensome regulation has focused on banks because banks bear much of the direct cost of regulation. In considering regulatory relief proposals, however, policymakers may want to consider not just the benefits of providing relief to small banks, but also the potential positive or negative effects that relief would have on consumers, market stability, and the safety and soundness of the banking system.

In some cases, congressional action is not necessary for small bank relief to occur in the future because regulators often have the authority to establish exemptions and to adjust the tailoring of rules. Without congressional action, however, exemptions and tailoring are likely to continue to occur on an ad hoc and inconsistent basis, for better or worse.

End Notes

[1] P.L. 111-203.

[2] For more information, see CRS Report R43081, *The Ability-to-Repay Rule: Possible Effects of the Qualified Mortgage Definition on Credit Availability and Other Selected Issues*, by Sean M. Hoskins.

[3] Because the operations of financial regulators are financed through fees and assessments on regulated institutions, any increase in the cost of conducting regulation may be passed on to banks.

[4] Gregory Elliehausen, *The Cost of Bank Regulation: A Review of the Evidence*, Board of Governors of the Federal Reserve System, April 1998, p. 3, at http://www.federalreserve.gov/pubs/staffstudies/1990-99/ss171.pdf.

[5] Foreign banks with certain U.S. charters are permitted to accept deposits and make loans in the United States, similar to a domestic bank. Other foreign banks are not, and are beyond the scope of this report.

[6] More specialized charters exist as well that are beyond the scope of this report.

[7] See, e.g., Board of Governors of the Federal Reserve System, *Community Banking*, at http://www.federalreserve.gov/ bankinforeg/topics/community_banking.htm.

[8] See, e.g., Office of the Comptroller of the Currency (OCC), *Community Bank Supervision: Comptroller's Handbook*, January 2010, at http://www.occ.treas.gov/publications/publications-by-type/comptrollers-handbook/cbs.pdf.

[9] See, e.g., Federal Deposit Insurance Corporation (FDIC), *FDIC Community Banking Study*, December 2012, at https://www.fdic.gov/regulations/resources/cbi/report/cbi-full.pdf.

[10] Thus, if the policy goal is to reduce regulatory burden on community banks rather than small banks, then the approaches discussed in this report based on bank size would not be the best way of achieving the policy goal.

[11] Congressional Research Service (CRS) estimate based on data from the FDIC, "Statistics on Depository Institutions," at https://www2.fdic.gov/sdi/. There are 449 banks with between $90 million and $110 million in assets that have a total of 11,270 full-time equivalent employees.

[12] CRS estimate based on data from the FDIC, "Statistics on Depository Institutions," at https://www2.fdic.gov/sdi/. There are 145 banks with between $900 million and $1.1billion in assets that have a total of 31,013 full-time equivalent employees.

[13] CRS estimate based on data from the FDIC, "Statistics on Depository Institutions," at https://www2.fdic.gov/sdi/. There are 17 banks with between $9 billion and $11 billion in assets that have a total of 19,941 full-time equivalent employees.

[14] See https://www.sba.gov/advocacy/firm-size-data. The SBA uses various different definitions of small business for eligibility for its programs. For more information, see CRS Report R40860, *Small Business Size Standards: A Historical Analysis of Contemporary Issues*, by Robert Jay Dilger.

[15] The head of a 2007 inter-agency study on regulatory burden stated that "it is difficult to accurately measure the impact regulatory burden has played in industry consolidation.... " Federal Financial Institutions Examination Council (FFIEC), *Joint Report to Congress: EGRPRA*," July 31, 2007, p. 3, at http://egrpra.ffiec.gov/docs/egrpra-jointreport.pdf. A 2014 study looked at the effect of regulatory burden on new charters and found that at least 75% of the decline could be attributed to macroeconomic conditions; see Robert M. Adams and Jacob P. Gramlich, *Where Are All the New Banks? The Role of Regulatory Burden in New Charter Creation*, Federal Reserve Board, December 16, 2014, at http://www.federalreserve.gov/econresdata/feds/2014/files/2014113pap.pdf.

[16] P.L. 103-328. For more on its effect on consolidation, U.S. Government Accountability Office (GAO), *Community Banks and Credit Unions: Impact of the Dodd-Frank Act Depends*

Largely on Future Rule Makings, GAO-12-881, September 2012, at http://www.gao.gov/assets/650/648210.pdf.

[17] The presence of economies of scale in banking has not been proven and is the subject of extensive research. See e.g., Federal Deposit Insurance Corporation, *FDIC Community Banking Study*, December 2012, pp. 5-22, at https://www.fdic.gov/regulations/resources/cbi/report/cbi-full.pdf.

[18] CRS Report RL33235, *Banking and Securities Regulation and Agency Enforcement Authorities*, by Mark Jickling et al.

[19] Fidelity Federal Savings and Loan Association v. De La Cuesta, 458 U.S. 141 (1982).

[20] For a full analysis, see CRS Report R43087, *Who Regulates Whom and How? An Overview of U.S. Financial Regulatory Policy for Banking and Securities Markets*, by Edward V. Murphy.

[21] Since the crises, some policymakers have emphasized systemic risk (macroprudential) regulation—the stability of the overall financial system—as distinct from safety and soundness (microprudential) regulation, which focuses on the stability of an individual institution. This topic is discussed in detail in the "Systemic Risk" section below.

[22] A completely unregulated system may result in both an unstable system and one in which there is a high cost of credit, however. Prudential regulation could therefore result in gains to both. Assuming that existing regulation has achieved a stable system, many argue that additional regulations are likely to lead to a tradeoff between the safety and stability of banks and the cost and availability of bank credit.

[23] For overview of shadow banking, see CRS Report R43345, *Shadow Banking: Background and Policy Issues*, by Edward V. Murphy.

[24] For additional information, see CRS Report R42572, *The Consumer Financial Protection Bureau (CFPB): A Legal Analysis*, by David H. Carpenter.

[25] P.L. 111-203, §1026.

[26] 12 U.S.C. 3208. For more information, see FFIEC, "About the FFIEC," at http://www.ffiec.gov/about.htm.

[27] FDIC Office of Inspector General, *The FDIC's Examination Process for Small Community Banks*, AUD-12-011, August 2012, p. 2, at http://www.fdicoig.gov/reports12/12-011AUD.pdf.

[28] See Federal Reserve System, Inspection Frequency and Scope Requirements for Bank Holding Companies and Savings and Loan Holding Companies with Total Consolidated Assets of $10 Billion or Less, SR 13-21, December 17, 2013, at http://www.federalreserve.gov/bankinforeg/srletters/sr1321.htm. CAMELS ratings are the rating system that serve as the basic safety and soundness standards used by bank regulators. For more information, see Jose A. Lopex, Using CAMELS Ratings to Monitor Bank Conditions, Federal Reserve Bank of San Francisco, June 1999, at http://www.frbsf.org/economic-research/publications/economic-letter/1999/june/using-camels-ratings-to-monitor-bankconditions/.

[29] CRS data query from FDIC's Statistics on Depository Institutions, available at https://www2.fdic.gov/sdi/index.asp.

[30] As of June 30, 2014. Source: http://www.americanbanker.com/rankings/cus-most-assets-1072621-1.html.

[31] Table 1.2 of https://www.fdic.gov/regulations/resources/cbi/report/cbi-full.pdf.

[32] CRS analysis of National Information Center, Bank Holding Company Peer Reports, fourth quarter of 2014, available at http://www.ffiec.gov/nicpubweb/content/BHCPRRPT/BHCPR_Peer.htm.

[33] Tanya Marsh and Joseph Norman, "The Impact of Dodd-Frank on Community Banks," American Enterprise Institute, white paper, 2013, p. 7, at https://www.stlouisfed.org/ banking/community-banking-conference/PDF/ Marsh_Norman_Reforming_Regulation.pdf.

[34] Gov. Daniel Tarullo, "A Tiered Approach to Regulation and Supervision of Community Banks," speech at the Community Bankers Symposium, Chicago, Illinois, November, 7, 2014, at http://www.federalreserve.gov/newsevents/ speech/tarullo20141107a.htm.

[35] Gov. Daniel Tarullo, "Rethinking the Aims of Prudential Regulation," speech at the Federal Reserve Bank of Chicago Bank Structure Conference, May 8, 2014, at http://www.federalreserve.gov/newsevents/speech/ tarullo20140508a.htm.

[36] Gov. Daniel Tarullo, "Rethinking the Aims of Prudential Regulation," speech at the Federal Reserve Bank of Chicago Bank Structure Conference, May 8, 2014, at http://www.federalreserve.gov/newsevents/speech/ tarullo20140508a.htm.

[37] Gov. Daniel Tarullo, "Rethinking the Aims of Prudential Regulation," speech at the Federal Reserve Bank of Chicago Bank Structure Conference, May 8, 2014, http://www.federal reserve.gov/newsevents/speech/ tarullo20140508a.htm.

[38] For more on the Volcker Rule, see CRS Report R43440, *The Volcker Rule: A Legal Analysis*, by David H. Carpenter and M. Maureen Murphy.

[39] For an introduction to the rulemaking process, see CRS Report IF10003, *Federal Regulations and the Rulemaking Process*, by Maeve P. Carey and Daniel T. Shedd.

[40] Gov. Daniel Tarullo, "A Tiered Approach to Regulation and Supervision of Community Banks," speech at the Community Bankers Symposium, Chicago, Illinois, November, 7, 2014, at http://www.federalreserve.gov/newsevents/ speech/tarullo20141107a.htm.

[41] For more on exemptions and tailoring, see Ron J. Feldman, *Supervision, Regulation, and Community Banks*, Federal Reserve Bank of Minneapolis, September 2014, at https://www.minneapolisfed.org/publications/banking-in-the-ninth/ supervision-regulation-and-community-banks.

[42] Appendix C to 12 C.F.R. §225. The threshold was raised in the 113th Congress from $500 million to $1 billion by P.L. 113-250, which was signed into law on December 18, 2014. The Fed issued a final rule on April 9, 2015 implementing this law.

[43] For more information, see CRS Report R42744, *U.S. Implementation of the Basel Capital Regulatory Framework*, by Darryl E. Getter.

[44] Technically, for purposes of reserve requirements, deposits are defined as "net transaction accounts," and include demand deposits and certain transfer accounts, but exclude deposits in savings accounts and time deposits. Transaction accounts are netted against certain cash due and in collection. For more information, see Federal Reserve System, "Reserve Requirements," at http://federalreserve.gov/monetarypolicy/reservereq.htm.

[45] 12 C.F.R. §363 and P.L. 107-204, §404. For more information, see FFIEC, *Joint Report to Congress: EGRPRA*, July 31, 2007, p. 30, at http://egrpra.ffiec.gov/docs/egrpra-joint-report.pdf.

[46] 5 U.S.C. §804(2).

[47] The Congressional Review Act "requires GAO to report to Congress on whether an agency, in promulgating a major rule, has complied with the regulatory process. GAO does not analyze or comment on the substance or quality of rulemaking. GAO's report must be made to each house of Congress no later than 15 calendar days after a rule's submission or publication date." GAO, "Congressional Review Act (CRA) FAQs," at http://www.gao.gov/legal/ congressact/cra_faq.html#3.

[48] For more information, see CRS Report R42150, *Systemically Important or "Too Big to Fail" Financial Institutions*, by Marc Labonte. Regulators also regulated and examined large,

complex banks differently before the Dodd-Frank enhanced prudential regime. For example, the Fed has issued a number of supervisory guidances that applied only to Large Complex Banking Organizations since the 1990s.

[49] For more information, see CRS Report IF00007, *Trust Preferred Securities (TruPS) (In Focus)*, by Edward V. Murphy.

[50] Those policy initiatives are Basel III, enhanced prudential regulation for systemically important financial institutions, the Volcker Rule, and debit card interchange fees.

[51] See Hester Peirce, *Scrap Regulations that Thin the Ranks of Small Banks*, Mercatus Center, George Mason University, February 23, 2015, at http://mercatus.org/expert_commentary/scrap-regulations-thin-ranks-small-banksdodd-frank.

[52] For more information, see CRS Report R41974, *Cost-Benefit and Other Analysis Requirements in the Rulemaking Process*, coordinated by Maeve P. Carey.

[53] As described in the section above "What is a Small Bank?"

[54] See Table 3 below for information on which major rules pursuant to the Dodd-Frank Act and Basel Accords have a significant economic impact on a substantial number of small entities under the Regulatory Flexibility Act (RFA).

[55] CRS Report R41974, *Cost-Benefit and Other Analysis Requirements in the Rulemaking Process*, coordinated by Maeve P. Carey, notes that "Section 1100G of the Dodd-Frank Act added a requirement to §603 of the RFA that for covered rules, the Consumer Financial Protection Bureau should include of a number of specific items in their impact analysis, including 'any projected increase in the cost of credit for small entities.'"

[56] P.L. 111-203, §1100G.

[57] 5 U.S.C. §603.

[58] For more on review panels, see CRS Report RL34355, *The Regulatory Flexibility Act: Implementation Issues and Proposed Reforms*, coordinated by Maeve P. Carey and CFPB, *Fact Sheet: Small Business Review Panel Process*, at http://files.consumerfinance.gov/f/201205_CFPB_public_factsheet-small-business-review-panel-process.pdf.

[59] See CRS Report RL34355, *The Regulatory Flexibility Act: Implementation Issues and Proposed Reforms*, coordinated by Maeve P. Carey.

[60] Federal Reserve Board, Office of the Inspector General, Board Should Enhance Compliance with Small Entity Compliance Guide Requirements Contained in the Small Business Regulatory Enforcement Fairness Act of 1996, July 1, 2013, Executive Summary, at http://oig.federalreserve.gov/reports/FRB_SBREFA_compliance_full_Jul2013.pdf.

[61] Federal Reserve Board Office of the Inspector General, Board Should Enhance Compliance with Small Entity Compliance Guide Requirements Contained in the Small Business Regulatory Enforcement Fairness Act of 1996, July 1, 2013, Executive Summary, at http://oig.federalreserve.gov/reports/FRB_SBREFA_compliance_full_Jul2013.pdf.

[62] OCC, Fed, FDIC, "Regulatory Publication and Review Under the Economic Growth and Regulatory Paperwork Reduction Act of 1996," 79 *Federal Register* 32173, June 4, 2014. Regulations under review can be found at FFIEC, "Regulations Under Review," at http://egrpra.ffiec.gov/regulations-under-review/regulations-under-review-index.html. The previous report can be accessed at FFIEC, *Joint Report to Congress: EGRPRA*, July 31, 2007, p. 30, at http://egrpra.ffiec.gov/docs/egrpra-joint-report.pdf.

[63] FDIC, "FDIC Law, Regulations, Related Acts: 5000 – Statements of Policy," at https://www.fdic.gov/regulations/ laws/rules/5000-400.html.

[64] Federal Reserve Board, *Annual Report 2013,* at http://www.federalreserve.gov/publications/annual-report/2013-supervision-and-regulation.htm#xbox4.easingregulatory burdenoncommun-99a70003.

[65] Federal Reserve System, *Community Banking Connections*, "Board Staff Perspective on Community Bank Supervision: One Size Doesn't Fit All," at https://www.community bankingconnections.org/articles/2014/Q2/viewfrom-washington.

[66] U.S. Congress, House Committee on Financial Services, *Testimony of Scott G. Alvarez, General Counsel of Federal Reserve*, 113th Cong., 2nd sess., April 8, 2014, at http://federal reserve.gov/newsevents/testimony/ alvarez20140408a.htm.

[67] FDIC, "FDIC Advisory Committee on Community Banking," at https://www.fdic.gov/ communitybanking/.

[68] Federal Reserve System, "Community Banking Connections," at https://www.community bankingconnections.org/.

[69] FDIC, "Community Banking Initiatives," at https://www.fdic.gov/regulations/ resources/ cbi/rtreport.html.

[70] OCC, *An Opportunity for Community Banks: Working Together Collaboratively,* January 13, 2015, at http://www.occ.gov/publications/publications-by-type/other-publications-reports/ pub-other-community-banksworking-collaborately.PDF.

[71] Gov. Tarullo discussed the possibility of "supervisory trickle down" for stress testing. See Gov. Daniel Tarullo, "A Tiered Approach to Regulation and Supervision of Community Banks," speech at the Community Bankers Symposium, Chicago, Illinois, November, 7, 2014, at http://www.federalreserve.gov/newsevents/speech/tarullo20141107a.htm.

[72] OCC, *Comptroller's Handbook*," at http://www.occ.gov/publications/publications-by-type/comptrollers-handbook/ index-comptrollers-handbook.html.

[73] Federal Reserve Board, *Annual Report 2013,* at http://www.federalreserve.gov/publications/ annual-report/2013-supervision-and-regulation.htm#xbox4.easingregulatoryburdenon commun-99a70003.

[74] Gov. Daniel Tarullo, "A Tiered Approach to Regulation and Supervision of Community Banks," speech at the Community Bankers Symposium, Chicago, Illinois, November, 7, 2014, at http://www.federalreserve.gov/newsevents/ speech/tarullo20141107a.htm.

[75] U.S. Congress, Senate Committee on Banking, Housing, and Urban Affairs, *Testimony of Ms. Doreen Eberley, FDIC*, 114th Cong., 1st sess., February 10, 2015.

[76] 12 C.F.R. §7.4000.

[77] For example, see Federal Reserve System, Inspection Frequency and Scope Requirements for Bank Holding Companies and Savings and Loan Holding Companies with Total Consolidated Assets of $10 Billion or Less, SR 13- 21, December 17, 2013, at http://www.federalreserve.gov/bankinforeg/srletters/sr1321.htm.

[78] See FFIEC, *Joint Report to Congress: EGRPRA*, July 31, 2007, p. 60, at http://egrpra.ffiec.gov/docs/egrpra-jointreport.pdf.

[79] See OCC, *OCC Bulletin 2013-15: Bank Appeals Process*, at http://www.occ.gov/news-issuances/bulletins/2013/ bulletin-2013-15.html.

[80] P.L. 103-325, §309.

[81] Gov.Daniel Tarullo, "A Tiered Approach to Regulation and Supervision of Community Banks," speech at the Community Bankers Symposium, Chicago, Illinois, November, 7, 2014, at http://www.federalreserve.gov/newsevents/ speech/tarullo20141107a.htm.

[82] U.S. Congress, Senate Committee on Banking, Housing, and Urban Affairs, *Testimony of Governor Daniel K. Tarullo, Federal Reserve*, 113th Cong., 2nd sess., September 9, 2014. More information on the pilot program is available at Federal Reserve System, "Federal Reserve Seeks to Conduct More Loan Reviews Off-Site," at https://www.community bankingconnections.org/articles/2014/q2/loan-reviews-off-site.

[83] U.S. Congress, Senate Committee on Banking, Housing, and Urban Affairs, *Testimony of Ms. Doreen R. Eberley,* FDIC, 113th Cong., 2nd sess., September 16, 2014.

[84] U.S. Congress, Senate Committee on Banking, Housing, and Urban Affairs, *Testimony of Ms. Doreen R. Eberley,* FDIC, 113th Cong., 2nd sess., September 16, 2014.

[85] Federal Reserve, "Small Bank Holding Company Policy Statement," press release, January 29, 2015, at http://www.federalreserve.gov/newsevents/press/bcreg/20150129b.htm.

[86] Gov. Daniel Tarullo, "A Tiered Approach to Regulation and Supervision of Community Banks," speech at the Community Bankers Symposium, Chicago, Illinois, November, 7, 2014, at http://www.federalreserve.gov/newsevents/ speech/tarullo20141107a.htm.

[87] An FDIC study found that community banks did not account for a disproportionate share of bank failures between 1975 and 2011, relative to their share of the industry. Because community banks account for more than 90% of organizations (by the FDIC definition, which as noted above is not limited to a size threshold), most bank failures are community banks, however. See FDIC, *FDIC Community Banking Study*, p. 2-10, December 2012, at https://www.fdic.gov/regulations/resources/cbi/report/cbi-full.pdf.

[88] See FDIC, *FDIC Community Banking Study*, p. B-2, December 2012, at https://www.fdic.gov/ regulations/resources/cbi/report/cbi-full.pdf.

[89] Data are for banks with high CAMELS rating. See FDIC Office of Inspector General, *The FDIC's Examination Process for Small Community Banks*, AUD-12-011, August 2012, at http://www.fdicoig.gov/reports12/12-011AUD.pdf.

[90] CFPB, *Understanding the Effects of Certain Deposit Regulations on Financial Institutions' Operations*, November 2013, p. 113, at http://files.consumerfinance.gov/f/201311_cfpb_ report_findings-relative-costs.pdf.

[91] Independent Community Bankers of America, *2014 ICBA Community Bank Call Report Burden Survey,* at http://icba.org/files/ICBASites/PDFs/2014CallReportSurveyResults.pdf.

[92] An alternative way to address this issue would be through activity-based regulation, instead of institution-based regulation with an exemption.

[93] Gov. Daniel Tarullo, "A Tiered Approach to Regulation and Supervision of Community Banks," speech at the Community Bankers Symposium, Chicago, Illinois, November, 7, 2014, at http://www.federalreserve.gov/newsevents/speech/tarullo20141107a.htm.

[94] See U.S. Government Accountability Office, *Community Banks and Credit Unions: Impact of the Dodd-Frank Act Depends Largely on Future Rule Makings*, GAO-12-881, September 2012, pp.14-19, at http://www.gao.gov/assets/650/ 648210.pdf. GAO defines small banks as banks having assets of $10 billion or less. One study found that until the mid-1990s local banks made relatively more small business loans in underserved areas, but in the late 1990s the trend reversed and they made relatively fewer. See Robert DeYoung, W. Scott Frame, and Dennis Glennon, et al., *Commercial Lending Distance and Historically Underserved Areas*, Federal Reserve Bank of Atlanta, July 2007, at https://www.frbatlanta.org/research/ publications/wp/2007/07_11.aspx.

[95] See FDIC, *FDIC Community Banking Study*, p. 3-6, December 2012, at https://www.fdic.gov/ regulations/resources/ cbi/report/cbi-full.pdf.

[96] For more information, see CRS Report R43081, *The Ability-to-Repay Rule: Possible Effects of the Qualified Mortgage Definition on Credit Availability and Other Selected Issues*, by Sean M. Hoskins.

[97] Tanya D. Marsh, "Reforming the Regulation of Community Banks After Dodd-Frank," *Indiana Law Journal*, vol. 90, no. 179, p. 19.

[98] See Conference of State Bank Supervisors, *An Incremental Approach to Financial Regulation: Right-Sized Regulations for Community Banks*, December 2013, at http://www.csbs.org/

legislative/testimony/Documents/An%20Incremental%20Approach%20to%20Financial%20Regulation.pdf.

[99] In portfolio lending, a bank holds the loan that it originated on its own books, so it retains the risks associated with the loan. By retaining the risk, some argue, the bank has greater incentive to make high-quality loans. See Conference of State Bank Supervisors, *An Incremental Approach to Financial Regulation: Right-Sized Regulations for Community Banks*, December 2013, at http://www.csbs.org/legislative/testimony/Documents/ An%20 Incremental%20Approach%20to%20Financial%20Regulation.pdf.

[100] Other, nongovernmental, sources have also analyzed the regulatory burden on small banks. For example, see Marshall Lux and Robert Greene, *The State and Fate of Community Banking*, Harvard Kennedy School, 2015, at http://www.hks.harvard.edu/centers/ mrcbg/publications/awp/awp37; KPMG, *2014 Banking Industry Outlook Survey*, at http://www.kpmginfo.com/industryoutlooksurveys/2014/pdfs/KPMGBankingIndustrySurvey_072414.pdf; Hester Peirce, Ian Robinson, and Thomas Stratmann, *How Are Small Banks Faring under Dodd-Frank?*, Mercatus Center, February 27, 2014, at http://mercatus.org/ publication/how-are-small-banks-faring-under-dodd-frank; Sam Batkins, *Dodd-Frank Fails at Measuring Costs and Benefits*, American Action Forum, February 19, 2015, at http://americanactionforum.org/insights/dodd-frank-fails-at-measuring-costs-and-benefits.

[101] FDIC, *FDIC Community Banking Study*, p. B-2, December 2012, at https://www.fdic.gov/ regulations/resources/cbi/ report/cbi-full.pdf.

[102] GAO, *Community Banks and Credit Unions: Impact of the Dodd-Frank Act Depends Largely on Future Rule Makings*, GAO-12-881, September 2012, pp.14-19, at http://www.gao.gov/ assets/650/648210.pdf.

[103] CFPB, *Understanding the Effects of Certain Deposit Regulations on Financial Institutions' Operations*, November 2013, p. 103, at http://files.consumerfinance.gov/f/201311_ cfpb_report_findings-relative-costs.pdf.

[104] CFPB, *Understanding the Effects of Certain Deposit Regulations on Financial Institutions' Operations*, November 2013, p. 113, at http://files.consumerfinance.gov/ f/201311_ cfpb_report_findings-relative-costs.pdf.

[105] CFPB, *Understanding the Effects of Certain Deposit Regulations on Financial Institutions' Operations*, November 2013, p. 6, at http://files.consumerfinance.gov/ f/201311_ cfpb_report_findings-relative-costs.pdf.

[106] Similarly, for all major rules, OMB reports by agency whether the agency provided "some information on benefits or costs." Between 2010 and 2013, it found that the banking regulators issued 17 major rules overall, of which the agencies reported "some information on benefits or costs" for 3 of those rules. In addition, the CFPB issued 6 major rules and provided some information on benefits or costs for all of them. See Table C-1 and C-2 of http://www.whitehouse.gov/sites/default/files/omb/inforeg/2014_cb/draft_2014_cost_benefit_report-updated.pdf.

[107] OCC and Federal Reserve System, "Regulatory Capital Rules," 78 *Federal Register* 62149, October 11, 2013 and FDIC, "Regulatory Capital Rules," 78 *Federal Register* 55340, September 10, 2013.

[108] Records can be accessed at http://www.reginfo.gov/public/do/PRASearch.

[109] Deputy Director Maryann Hunter, Federal Reserve, testimony before the U.S. Senate, Committee on Banking, Housing, And Urban Affairs, February 10, 2015, transcript from http://www.cq.com/doc/congressionaltranscripts4623253?4.

[110] Department of the Treasury, Office of Inspector General, *Safety and Soundness: Review of OCC Community Bank Examination and Appeals Processes*, August 31, 2012, at

http://www.treasury.gov/about/organizational-structure/ig/Audit%20Reports%20and%20 Testimonies/OIG12070.pdf.

[111] See FDIC, Office of Inspector General, *The FDIC's Examination Process for Small Community Banks*, AUD-12- 011, p. 8, August 2012, at http://www.fdicoig.gov/reports12/ 12-011AUD.pdf.

[112] Federal Reserve System, Office of Inspector General, *Audit of the Small Community Bank Examination Process*, p. 18, August 2012, at http://oig.federalreserve.gov/reports/ Audit_SCB_Exam_Process_August2012.pdf.

[113] Independent Community Bankers of America (ICBA), *2014 ICBA Community Bank Call Report Burden Survey*, at http://www.icba.org/files/ICBASites/PDFs/2014CallReport SurveyResults.pdf.

[114] For example, the Financial Stability Board and Basel Committee provided macroeconomic estimates of the effects of implementing Basel III capital standards. See Macroeconomic Assessment Group, *Assessing the Macroeconomic Impact of the Transition to Stronger Capital and Liquidity Requirements*, Dec. 2010, http://www.bis.org/publ/ othp12.pdf.

[115] H.R. 1599, the Community Institution Mortgage Relief Act of 2015, for example, would (among other things) direct the CFPB to raise its small servicer exemption in a mortgage servicing rule to include servicers that service 20,000 or fewer mortgage loans from the current 5,000 loan threshold.

[116] This model would not apply a standard exemption to all regulations, or else all banks subject to the exemption would be completely unregulated.

[117] In an interview with *American Banker,* Sheila Bair, former chairman of the FDIC, suggested a $10 billion threshold for broad exemptions and tailoring. See Rob Blackwell, "The Easy Legislative Fix that Could Save Community Banks," *American Banker*, February 23, 2015.

[118] For a review of the erosion of differences between banks and thrifts, see Dain Donelson and David Zaring, "Requiem for a Regulator," *North Carolina Law Review*, 2011, vol. 89, p. 1777, at http://www.nclawreview.org/ documents/89/5/zaring.pdf; "Transfer of Powers to the Comptroller of the Currency, the Corporation, and the Board of Governors," *Review of Banking and Financial Law*, Issue I, Fall 2010, Ch. IX, http://www.bu.edu/rbfl/ files/2013/09/TransferOfPowers.pdf.

[119] The Office of Thrift Supervision's (OTS's) performance during the financial crisis is reviewed in U.S. Congress, Senate Committee on Homeland Security and Governmental Affairs, Permanent Subcommittee on Investigations, *Wall Street and the Financial Crisis, Majority and Minority Staff Report*, 112th Cong., 1st sess., April 13, 2011, chap. 4. For an additional perspective, see Dain Donelson and David Zaring, "Requiem for a Regulator," *North Carolina Law Review*, 2011, vol. 89, p. 1777, at http://www.nclawreview.org/ documents/89/5/zaring.pdf; "Transfer of Powers to the Comptroller of the Currency, the Corporation, and the Board of Governors," *Review of Banking and Financial Law*, Issue I, Fall 2010, Ch. IX, http://www.bu.edu/rbfl/files/2013/09/TransferOfPowers.pdf.

[120] Assuming economies of scale to compliance effects do not dominate.

In: Bank Regulation
Editor: Miranda Schmidt
ISBN: 978-1-63485-520-4

Chapter 3

A TIERED APPROACH TO REGULATION AND SUPERVISION OF COMMUNITY BANKS*

Daniel K. Tarullo

Earlier this year—also speaking to a conference at the Federal Reserve Bank of Chicago —I explained the need for an explicitly tiered approach to banking regulation and supervision.1 Today I would like to elaborate on those earlier remarks to suggest in more detail what a tiered approach would mean for community banks. Let me begin, though, by recapitulating my basic premise and the reasoning behind it.

RATIONALE FOR REGULATORY TIERING

For more than 75 years following passage of the Banking Act of 1933, the motivation for banking regulation was fairly simple: the government had granted deposit insurance and access to the discount window to depository institutions to forestall runs and panics. The resulting moral hazard and the use of insured deposits as a funding source for these institutions justified prudential measures, including prohibitions on non-banking activities, aimed at maintaining safe and sound banks, which would in turn protect taxpayers.

* This is an edited, reformatted and augmented version of a speech given at the Community Bankers Symposium, Chicago, Illinois on November 7, 2014. Daniel K. Tarullo is a member of the Board of Governors of the Federal Reserve System.

Prudential regulation of bank holding companies by the Federal Reserve under authority granted by the Bank Holding Company Act of 1956 was aimed primarily at protecting insured depository institutions and the federal deposit insurance fund from knock-on effects of problems at affiliated nonbank businesses.

This approach is what we now characterize as microprudential—that is, the focus is on the soundness of individual banks rather than on the financial system more broadly. This is not to say that financial stability had not been important to financial regulators, but this stability was implicitly assumed to follow from having sound individual banks.

Over the years, of course, banking regulation evolved. For example, regulation expanded to encompass fair and open access to financial services for consumers. And, as developments in financial markets and deregulation over the past several decades led to a more concentrated financial sector in which bank holding companies could engage in a much broader range of activities, supervision was tiered within the bank regulatory agencies based on the size and complexity of the regulated institutions. But the financial crisis provoked a fundamental rethink of the aims of prudential regulation.

There is now more widespread agreement that these aims should vary according to the size, scope, and range of activities of banking organizations. Most significantly, banks of a size and complexity such that serious stress or failure could pose risks to the entire financial system need regulation that incorporates the macroprudential aim of protecting financial stability.[2] There is also a good argument that very large banks that fall short of this level of systemic importance should nonetheless be regulated with an eye to macroprudential aims, such as the ability of the banking system as a whole to provide credit.

Although individual community banks may be an important source of credit, particularly in local economies outside urban areas, neither systemic risk nor broad macroprudential considerations are significant in thinking about prudential regulation of community banks. So what *should* the aims of such regulation be? The basic answer is it should protect the deposit insurance fund. In other words, the traditional microprudential approach to safety and soundness regulation continues to be appropriate for these banks. To develop that basic answer, I think it useful to begin with an understanding of both the business model of community banks—that is, how their financial intermediation adds value to the economy—and the ways in which such banks are most likely to encounter problems.

There are roughly 5,700 community banks in the United States, the vast majority of which have less than $1 billion in total assets.[3] These banks represent 98 percent of insured U.S. commercial banks, but collectively hold just under 20 percent of aggregate banking assets. Moreover, the business model of most community banks, especially smaller and rural banks, is built substantially on relationship banking. While community banks have over the years found it increasingly difficult to compete with larger banks in types of lending that can be efficiently scaled through larger volumes and standardized credit models, they maintain a comparative advantage relative to larger competitors through knowledge of their local communities and their individual borrowers.[4] This means that community banks play a unique role in their local economies, particularly with regard to lending to small- and medium-sized businesses.

Numerous studies have documented this advantage and its value to economic development. One recent study found that loans extended by rural community banks to small businesses default less frequently than similar loans granted by their urban counterparts, and that the performance advantage is greater when the bank and the borrower are located in the same county. This finding suggests that the "soft" information obtained from their local relationships usefully informs rural community banks' underwriting.[5] Federal Reserve research also suggests that many community banks that adhered to the traditional relationship banking model of funding local lending with customer deposits continued to thrive even during the worst years of the financial crisis.[6]

In contrast, many small banks that turned to a more transactional model and funded construction loans—often outside of their local market—with borrowings, rather than core deposits, failed. And, precisely because of their business model, community banks do have their vulnerabilities. They are more likely to have geographic and portfolio concentrations that can make them vulnerable to localized economic problems. Of course, the failure of a community bank in these circumstances will only exacerbate these problems. Especially in rural areas, the disappearance of community banks could result in a permanent reduction in this local kind of credit, as the slack may not all be picked up by larger banks.[7] Additionally, of course, there will usually be issues requiring supervisory and management consideration for at least a time. At present, as I know you have been hearing from your supervisors, these issues include cybersecurity and interest rate risks.

To return, then, to the aims of prudential regulation of community banks, it seems that we can fill out the basic aims of protecting the deposit insurance fund and supporting the availability of relationship lending across the country by concentrating on traditional capital regulation to ensure solvency and on traditional examination practice to monitor the basic soundness of the relationship lending practices. We may also need to increase scrutiny when community banks move beyond their traditional business model and enter lines or markets that are more complex or with which they may not be familiar. But many rules and examinations that are important for institutions that are larger, more complex, or both, do not make sense in light of the nature of the risks to community banks. We must avoid importing measures from large bank oversight that make relationship banking more costly.

With that explanation of the purposes of community bank oversight, let me now turn to more specific discussion of how we are tailoring regulation and supervision of community banks to achieve those aims.

Tiered Regulation for Community Banks

There are two complementary ways to implement a tiered approach to prudential regulation. One is to apply specific regulations only to those classes of banking organizations whose activities and scale require those measures. The second is to tailor the application of generally applicable measures based on the size, complexity, and possibly other characteristics of banking organizations. We are following both approaches in putting into place an explicitly tiered method of regulating community banks.[8]

An example of tailoring generally applicable regulations is the revised capital guidelines that were issued in 2013.[9] It was clear in the wake of the financial crisis that strong capital positions were essential for banks of all sizes, including community banks. But a number of changes that were appropriate for large banks did not make sense for community banks. As I am sure you all recall, community banks gave us quite a bit of help in identifying which portions of the originally proposed rule were, and were not, appropriate for community banks. Following publication of the final capital rule, the three federal banking agencies developed a streamlined, supplemental *Community Bank Guide* to assist bank management in understanding the applicability of the rules to smaller, non-complex institutions.[10] This exercise is an example of a broader effort to be explicit as to how prudential regulations that are sometimes quite detailed apply to community banks. By including such explanations in the introductory portions of broadly applicable regulations, our hope is that community bankers will be relieved of the task of wading through extensive regulatory texts just to find out what portions apply to their banks.

This is a good point at which to note that the federal banking agencies have, in accordance with the terms of the Economic Growth and Regulatory Paperwork Reduction Act (EGRPRA), recently launched a review to identify banking regulations that are outdated, unnecessary, or unduly burdensome.[11] One theme that has already been notable is the belief of community bankers that many regulations could be tailored more appropriately for community banks. I encourage you to participate in the EGRPRA process by giving us specific examples of regulations that should be modified in this way and, even more helpfully, by suggesting specific ways in which they might be usefully be tailored. [12]

As to exempting community banks entirely from certain regulations, I should note first that many of the statutory requirements introduced by the Dodd-Frank Wall Street Reform and Consumer Protection Act do not by their own terms apply to community banks. So, for example, the extensive enhanced prudential standards required by section 165 of Dodd-Frank for bank holding companies with more than $50 billion in assets do not apply to smaller banks. Nor do the requirements for stress testing and resolution planning.[13] Similarly, the banking agencies have used their discretion to exclude community banks from the coverage of some new regulations adopted following the crisis. For example, we recently approved a final rule implementing in the United States a Basel agreement that establishes a quantitative minimum liquidity requirement, but limited its coverage to banking organizations with more than $50 billion in assets.[14] We excluded community and smaller regional banks, which generally have relatively simple funding profiles and do not pose a significant potential risk to the financial system.

However, some statutory requirements by their terms apply to all banks. Even if we do not believe that they actually advance safety and soundness aims for community banks, or produce only a small benefit at a disproportionately large compliance cost, we must still enforce them. It would be worthwhile to consider amendments to these statutory provisions to carve out their applicability to community banks.

I have previously suggested two candidates for consideration: the Volcker rule and the incentive compensation requirements in section 956 of Dodd-Frank.[15] The risks addressed by these statutory provisions are far more significant at larger institutions than they are at community banks.[16] Moreover, in the unlikely event that a community bank engages in practices in either of these areas that raise heightened concerns, we would be able to address these concerns as part of the normal safety-and-soundness supervisory process. While the banking agencies have used the other method of tiering and tried to tailor the Volcker rule (as we will do with section 956), I believe that both community banks and supervisors would benefit from not having to focus on formal compliance with regulation of matters that are unlikely to pose problems at smaller banks.

Today I would like to add a third candidate for consideration—a statutory amendment that would permit the Federal Reserve Board to raise the size of banks covered by our Small Bank Holding Company Policy Statement.[17] As background, the Board originally issued the policy statement in 1980 to facilitate the transfer of ownership of small community banks. The Board generally discourages the use of debt by bank holding companies to finance acquisitions, because debt can impair the ability of the holding company to serve as a source of strength to subsidiary banks. However, the Board also recognizes that limited access to equity funding by small institutions means that the transfer of ownership of small banks often requires the use of acquisition debt.

The policy statement allows small, noncomplex bank holding companies to operate with higher levels of debt than would normally be permitted, subject to restrictions to ensure that higher debt does not pose an undue risk to subsidiary banks and that leverage is reduced over time. Bank holding companies that are subject to the policy statement are exempt from the Board's risk-based and leverage capital guidelines, and are subject to reduced regulatory reporting requirements.[18]

The original policy statement set the maximum size of qualifying holding companies at $150 million in total consolidated assets. This threshold was increased to $500 million in 2006 to address the effects of inflation, industry consolidation, and asset growth. The intervening eight years have obviously brought dramatic changes in the financial, business, and regulatory environments. Accordingly, I believe it is worth considering raising the asset threshold once again, this time to $1 billion. Approximately 85 percent of all bank holding companies qualified after the threshold was raised in 2006, a figure that has dropped to about 75 percent today. Raising the threshold to $1 billion would recoup that lost coverage and go a bit further, covering 89 percent of holding companies.

Such an increase would entail some policy tradeoffs, of course, which obviously become of greater concern as the threshold rises further. But I think the balance of considerations argues for taking this action to facilitate transfers of ownership of small banks. For example, while exempting more bank holding companies could result in increased leverage, subsidiary banks remain subject to normal capital requirements. Supervisory and applications approval processes are available to limit instances in which holding companies could take on excessive debt. Similarly, because most bank holding companies under $1 billion have limited activities outside of their banks, and we will still receive detailed quarterly bank data, the reduced regulatory reporting requirements for qualifying holding companies should not be problematic for supervisors.

Of course, the policy statement was issued by the Board and thus one might think the Board could raise the threshold on its own. However, the Collins amendment to Dodd-Frank[19] effectively eliminates any authority of the Board to extend the capital treatment in the policy statement to holding companies with assets greater than the threshold in effect on May 19, 2010, or to savings and loan holding companies of any size. Thus, we would need legislative action to effect these changes.

TIERED SUPERVISION

Federal banking regulators have long organized supervision into portfolios of institutions based predominantly—though for larger firms, not exclusively—on asset size. Various provisions of Dodd-Frank motivated the Federal Reserve to modify the composition of the portfolios somewhat. We have four such groups: (1) community banks, (2) regional banking organizations, (3) large banking organizations, and (4) firms overseen by the Large Institution Supervision Coordinating Committee (LISCC).[20] This arrangement is not simply a matter of organizational convenience. Nor is it only a means for promoting consistency of treatment among similar banks throughout the Federal Reserve System, important as that goal is. As with tiered regulation, this tiered approach to supervision is intended to take account of differences in business models, risks, relative regulatory burden, and other salient considerations. Where specific regulatory goals for the different portfolios vary, the supervisory programs should reflect those differences. And where the goals are similar across portfolios, supervisory programs should take account of the differences among banks noted a moment ago. A tiered approach to prudential regulation calls not for a single state of the art in supervision, but for distinct state-of-the-art approaches to each supervisory portfolio. Some important implications for community bank supervision follow from this principle.

First, the characteristics and business model of community banks must be reflected in the supervisory program. Detailed rules, regulations, and supervisory expectations are clearly needed at times for overseeing the systems created in large, geographically dispersed organizations where the distance from head office to operating branches can be very far indeed. But in a well-run community bank where the president may oversee a relatively small staff and can communicate and enforce expectations and standards face-to-face, some kinds of supervisory expectations needed for larger banks may be unnecessary. In fact, such supervision can be burdensome, because community banks have a smaller balance sheet across which to amortize compliance costs. Such rules can also sometimes conflict with the flexibility that is important to community banks meeting their customers' needs. For instance, community banks should readily comply with expectations that they extend credit on safe and sound terms. However, to the extent that supervisors dictate the precise details of what terms are safe and sound, banks may find it more difficult to structure a loan in a way that matches a borrower's needs or credit situation. This can result in a lessening of credit availability and economic activity. Attention to a bank's practices in making its relationship lending decisions, and on the performance of the loans that have been made, may be supervisory time better spent.

A similar observation can be made with respect to consumer compliance supervision of community banks, for which the Federal Reserve implemented a new examination program in January 2014.[21] While we have traditionally applied a risk-focused approach to consumer compliance examinations, the new program more explicitly links examination intensity to the individual community bank's risk profile. Here again, the scale of community banks is directly relevant to supervisory choices. Community banks do not have large, standardized systems for dealing with many customers across a far-flung geographic footprint. They *do* have much more direct contact between customers and bank management. The new program calls for examiners to spend less time on low-risk compliance issues at community banks. In addition, we revised our consumer compliance examination frequency policy to lengthen the time between on-site consumer compliance and Community Reinvestment Act examinations for many community banks with less than $1 billion in total consolidated assets.

A second implication of supervisory tiering is that supervision must not inadvertently undo the decisions made through regulatory tiering. This point raises the oft-cited concern about "supervisory trickle down," whereby supervisory expectations—or even regulatory requirements—formulated for larger banks are de facto applied in part to community banks. The concern has been particularly acute in the context of capital stress testing, though it is by no means limited to that area. Let me repeat here what all three federal banking agencies have explained in the clearest possible terms, both publicly, in examiner training, and in one-on-one discussions with bankers: that Dodd-Frank Act Stress Test (DFAST) and Comprehensive Capital Analysis and Review requirements and expectations for enterprise-wide capital stress testing do not apply to community banking organizations, either explicitly or implicitly.[22] For example, while it may be sensible supervisory practice to inquire of a growing $9 billion bank if it has begun thinking about how it would meet DFAST requirements should it reach the current $10 billion statutory threshold, that bank does not need to start meeting those requirements until it has actually crossed the threshold. And there is simply no reason for examiners to make a $5 billion bank begin to develop capital stress testing capabilities.

Third, the relatively straightforward business model of community banks, along with their relatively small scale and number of branches, provides the opportunity to increase the use of off-site supervisory oversight, in accordance with informing principles of risk-based supervision. For example, last year we pilot-tested a voluntary program under which some aspects of the loan review process were conducted off-site, relying on the bank's electronic records to assess loan quality and underwriting practices. Overall, community bankers that were part of the pilot expressed strong support for this approach, which reduced the time examiners needed to spend on-site at bank offices. As a result, we plan to continue using this approach in future examinations at qualified banks that maintain electronic loan records and wish to participate in this approach. This initiative could tangibly reduce burden on community banking organizations.

More generally, the Federal Reserve has invested substantial resources in developing technological tools for examiners to improve the efficiency of both off-site and on-site supervisory activities. These tools should lead to greater consistency and more efficient, effective, and risk-focused examinations as they assist staff in tailoring the scope of examinations to the activities and risks at individual banks. The automation of various parts of the community bank examination process can also save examiners and bank management time, as a bank can submit requested pre-examination information electronically rather than mailing paper copies to a Federal Reserve Bank.

These observations relate to another issue that I might note in passing. As you know, there have been questions raised as to whether the level of required reporting is itself a regulatory burden that might be mitigated for small banks. The banking agencies are considering these issues under the auspices of the Federal Financial Institutions Examination Council. I do think there may be some opportunities to streamline the content or frequency of reporting for smaller banks. However, I would observe that many of the efficiency improvements that I have previously described were dependent on the data collected each quarter in Call Reports. For example, the availability of this data was a factor in raising the threshold for eligibility for the 18-month examination cycle from $250 million to $500 million. Similarly, the regular Call Report data for subsidiary banks buttress the case for increasing the threshold for application of the Small Bank Holding Company Policy Statement. Thus, there may be some tradeoffs among various possible simplifying supervisory measures.

CONCLUSION

As I noted in my speech six months ago, the old unitary approach to prudential oversight has in practical terms been supplanted by various statutory, regulatory, and supervisory measures, particularly since the financial crisis. Tiered regulation and supervision is a reality. My hope is that by acknowledging and, indeed, applauding that reality, legislators and prudential regulators can shape an oversight regime that most effectively realizes the complementary goals of banking soundness, financial stability, and economic growth. Post-crisis attention has understandably been focused on too-big-to-fail issues and other sources of systemic risk. But now is a good time to look at the other end of the banking industry, where the contrast is substantial. Smaller banks present a very different set of business models. Their risks and vulnerabilities tend to grow from different sources. An explicit and sustained tailoring of regulation and supervision for community banks not only seems reasonable, it seems an important and logical next step in financial regulatory reform.

End Notes

[1] Daniel K. Tarullo (2014), "Rethinking the Aims of Prudential Regulation," speech delivered at the Federal Reserve Bank of Chicago Bank Structure Conference, Chicago, May 8, www.federalreserve.gov/newsevents/speech/tarullo20140508a.htm. See also Janet L. Yellen

(2014), "Tailored Supervision of Community Banks," speech delivered at the Independent Community Bankers of America 2014 Washington Policy Summit, Washington, D.C., May 1, www.federalreserve.gov/newsevents/speech/yellen20140501a.htm; Jerome H. Powell (2014), introductory remarks delivered at the Federal Reserve/Conference of State Bank Supervisors Community Banking Research Conference, St. Louis, Missouri, September 23, www.federalreserve.gov/newsevents/speech/powell20140923a.htm; and Elizabeth A. Duke (2012), "Opportunities to Reduce Regulatory Burden and Improve Credit Availability," speech delivered to the 2012 Bank Presidents Seminar, Santa Barbara, California, January 13, www.federalreserve.gov/newsevents/speech/duke20120113a.htm.

[2] For additional thoughts on the importance of a macroprudential approach, see Daniel K. Tarullo (2013), "Macroprudential Regulation," speech delivered at the Yale Law School Conference on Challenges in Global Financial Services, New Haven, Connecticut, September 20, at www.federalreserve.gov/newsevents/speech/tarullo20130920a.htm; and Ben S. Bernanke (2011), "Implementing a Macroprudential Approach to Supervision and Regulation," speech delivered at the 47th Annual Conference on Bank Structure and Competition, Chicago, May 5, at www.federalreserve.gov/newsevents/speech/ bernanke20110505a.htm.

[3] For supervisory purposes, the Federal Reserve typically defines community banks as those with $10 billion or less in total assets. In addition, these remarks will refer to both "community banks" and "community banking organizations." While the former typically refers to depository institutions and the latter refers to banking groups more generally, including holding companies, for purposes of my remarks today these are used interchangeably unless indicated otherwise.

[4] Of course, larger banks may also devote important parts of their business to relationship lending, but it is sometimes suggested that, even so, smaller banks whose management is present in local communities are better adapted to relationship lending business models.

[5] See Robert DeYoung, Dennis Glennon, Peter Nigro, and Kenneth Spong (2012), "Small Business Lending and Social Capital: Are Rural Relationships Different?" University of Kansas Center for Banking Excellence Research Paper #2012-1, June, business.ku.edu/sites/businessdev.drupal.ku.edu/files/docs/CBE%20WP%202012-1%20DeYoung%20Glennon%20Nigro%20Spong.pdf.

[6] See, for example, R. Alton Gilbert, Andrew P. Meyer, and James W. Fuchs (2013), "The Future of Community Banks: Lessons from Banks That Thrived During the Recent Financial Crisis," Federal Reserve Bank of St. Louis Review, vol. 95 (March/April), pp. 115–143, research.stlouisfed.org/publications/review/13/02/gilbert.pdf; and Dean F. Amel and Robin A. Prager (2014), "Community Bank Performance: How Important are Managers?" Finance and Economics Discussion Series 2014-26 (Washington: Board of Governors of the Federal Reserve System, March 18), www.federalreserve.gov/ pubs/feds/2014/201426/201426pap.pdf. For a study finding relationship lending benefits in an international context, see Franco Fiordelisi, Stefano Monferra, and Gabriele Sampagnaro (2014), "Relationship Lending and Credit Quality," Journal of Financial Services Research, vol. 46, pp. 295–315.

[7] Counties that experience failures of community banks are likely to see significantly lower income and compensation growth, higher poverty rates, and lower employment. See John Kandrac (2013), "Bank Failure, Relationship Lending, and Local Economic Performance," www.stlouisfed.org/banking/community-bankingconference/PDF/Kandrac BankFailure CBRC2013.pdf.

[8] While not directly the subject of these remarks, it also bears noting that additional tiering of expectations is increasingly taking place even among larger banking organizations. For

example, capital planning and stress testing requirements are more extensive for the very largest, most systemically important firms than they are for smaller regional banking organizations. Likewise, liquidity and capital requirements are or will be higher for the most systemically important firms than for other large banking organizations.

[9] See Federal Deposit Insurance Corporation (FDIC) (2013), "Regulatory Capital Rules: Regulatory Capital, Implementation of Basel III, Capital Adequacy, Transition Provisions, Prompt Corrective Action, Standardized Approach for Risk-Weighted Assets, Market Discipline and Disclosure Requirements, Advanced Approaches Risk-Based Capital Rule, and Market Risk Capital Rule," interim final rule, Federal Register, vol. 78, pp. 55340–55598, www.fdic.gov/news/board/2013/2013-07-09_notice_dis_a_res.pdf; and Board of Governors of the Federal Reserve System (Board of Governors) and Office of the Comptroller of the Currency (OCC) (2013), final rule of the same name, Federal Register, vol. 78, pp. 62017–62291, www.gpo.gov/fdsys/pkg/FR-2013-10-11/pdf/2013-21653.pdf.

[10] Board of Governors, FDIC, and OCC (2013), New Capital Rule: Community Bank Guide (Washington: Board of Governors, FDIC, and OCC, July), www.federalreserve.gov/bankinforeg/basel/files/capital_rule_community_bank_guide_20130709.pdf.

[11] Board of Governors, FDIC, and OCC (2014), "Federal Bank Regulatory Agencies Seek Comment on Interagency Effort to Reduce Regulatory Burden," press release, June 4, www.federalreserve.gov/newsevents/press/bcreg/20140604a.htm. See also the Federal Financial Institutions Examination Council's (FFIEC) EGRPRA website at http://egrpra.ffiec.gov/.

[12] See http://egrpra.ffiec.gov/.

[13] For more information about large-bank capital planning and stress testing requirements, see the Board's website at www.federalreserve.gov/bankinforeg/stress-tests-capital-planning.htm.

[14] Board of Governors, OCC, and FDIC (2014), "Liquidity Coverage Ratio: Liquidity Risk Measurement Standards," final rule, Federal Register, vol. 79 (October 10), pp. 61439–61541, www.gpo.gov/fdsys/pkg/FR-2014- 10-10/pdf/2014-22520.pdf.

[15] The Volcker rule applies to all banking entities that engage in prohibited activities, irrespective of size, and the Dodd-Frank incentive compensation requirements apply to all banks and holding companies with total assets of $1 billion or more.

[16] As indicated in guidance for community banks that was issued with the final Volcker rule, in practice the agencies believe that the vast majority of community banks do not engage in prohibited activities. Because they are not expressly exempted from the Volcker rule provisions, however, if community bankers have any questions about whether their bank engages in prohibited activities, they may feel obliged to conduct due diligence on a very complex rule. Given the limited de facto applicability to community banks, I would suggest that exempting them from Volcker compliance and resolving issues through the supervisory process would be a more effective use of bank and supervisory resources. See Board of Governors, FDIC, and OCC (2013), "The Volcker Rule: Community Bank Applicability," December 10, www.federalreserve.gov/newsevents/press/bcreg/bcreg20131210a4.pdf.

[17] See 12 CFR part 225, appendix C, www.gpo.gov/fdsys/pkg/CFR-2014-title12-vol3/pdf/CFR-2014-title12-vol3- part225-appC.pdf.

[18] Bank holding companies with less than $500 million in assets may still be required to file regulatory reports with the same detail and frequency as larger bank holding companies if they meet certain criteria that are set forth in the instructions for the Federal Reserve FR Y-9SP and FR Y-9C regulatory reports (www.federalreserve.gov/apps/reportforms/default.aspx) or to otherwise meet supervisory needs.

[19] Section 171 of the Dodd-Frank Act.

[20] Community banking organizations generally are those with $10 billion or less in total assets, regional banking organizations are those with total assets between $10 billion and $50 billion, large banking organizations are those with total assets over $50 billion, and LISCC firms are the subset of large banking organizations that are largest and most systemically important. For more information on the LISCC, including the firms currently in the LISCC portfolio, see the Board's website at www.federalreserve.gov/bankinforeg/large-institution-supervision.htm.

[21] Board of Governors, Division of Consumer and Community Affairs (2013), "Community Bank Risk-Focused Consumer Compliance Supervision Program," Consumer Affairs Letter CA 13-19 (November 18); and "Consumer Compliance and Community Reinvestment Act (CRA) Examination Frequency Policy," Consumer Affairs Letter CA 13-20 (November 18).

[22] See, for example, Board of Governors, FDIC, and OCC (2012), "Statement to Clarify Supervisory Expectations for Stress Testing by Community Banks," May 14, www.federalreserve.gov/newsevents/press/bcreg/20120514b.htm.

INDEX

C

G

H

I

R

S

T

U

V

W